Accession no.

D1329313

# Complaint
## psychothe

This handbook has been written to help individuals and organizations offering psychotherapy and counselling manage complaints and grievances. It shows how the necessary processes and procedures can be ordered within a framework of natural justice on an ethically sound basis.

Fiona Palmer Barnes draws on her own extensive experience of managing complaints to explore the role of organizations in establishing good practice. She develops the notion of the competent, ethical practitioner and looks at this in terms of the limits of confidentiality in the work and the making of a therapeutic contract. The situations which are likely to lead to grievances are also examined.

Through a number of vignettes the reader is guided through the processing of a complaint from the moment it is made, the investigatory and adjudicatory procedures, to a final outcome. Sanctions and appeals are also illustrated. The book includes the Codes of Ethics and Complaints Procedures of the major UK organizations in psychotherapy, psychology and counselling and is an essential guide to the handling of these procedures for all practitioners.

**Fiona Palmer Barnes** is an analytical psychologist in private practice in Herefordshire and currently chairs the Ethics Committee of the United Kingdom Council for Psychotherapy. She is past chair of the Complaints Committee of the British Association for Counselling.

# Complaints and grievances in psychotherapy

## A handbook of ethical practice

Fiona Palmer Barnes

LIBRARY

| ACC. No. | DEPT. |

CLASS No.
616.8914 PAL

UNIVERSITY
COLLEGE CHESTER

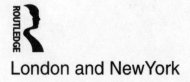

London and New York

First published 1998 by Routledge
11 New Fetter Lane, London EC4P 4EE

Simultaneously published in the USA and Canada
by Routledge
29 West 35th Street, New York, NY 10001

© 1998 Fiona Palmer Barnes

Typeset in Times by Keystroke, Jacaranda Lodge, Wolverhampton
Printed and bound in Great Britain by Clays Ltd, St Ives PLC

All rights reserved. No part of this book may be reprinted or
reproduced or utilized in any form or by any electronic,
mechanical, or other means, now known or hereafter
invented, including photocopying and recording, or in any
information storage or retrieval system, without permission in
writing from the publishers.

*British Library Cataloguing in Publication Data*
A catalogue record for this book is available from the British Library

*Library of Congress Cataloguing in Publication Data*
A catalogue record for this book has been requested

ISBN 0–415–15250–X (hbk)
ISBN 0–415–15251–8 (pbk)

*To Miles and Guy*

# Contents

# Acknowledgements

I would have been unable to write this book without the experience I have gained through working on committees and with organizational members of the British Association for Counselling and the United Kingdom Council for Psychotherapy. Particularly, I would like to acknowledge the contribution of Alan Jamieson, with whom I have worked for over fifteen years in writing codes of ethics and, more recently, in managing matters of complaint. Our discussions and his thoughts have contributed considerably to the concept of this book.

I most gratefully acknowledge the help of Rosemary Rollason of Walker Martineau for reading the final draft. Also Judith Baron, Ann Casement, Gordon Law, Susie Lendrum, Leslie Murdin, Sandy Murray and Gabrielle Syme, who have read parts, or the whole, of drafts of the book and whose comments have been invaluable. I would also like to thank Annie Macdonald who gave me comfort and encouraged me to write.

I am grateful to the British Association for Counselling, the British Psychological Society, the British Confederation of Psychotherapists and the United Kingdom Council of Psychotherapy for their permission to reproduce their Guidelines or Codes of Ethics and their Complaints Procedures in the appendices.

My heartfelt thanks go to Andrew Samuels for the most generous of forewords and to Hilary Engel who edited the drafts and really helped me give shape to the book. She continued to encourage me at the bleaker moments.

Finally to Neil without whose care and support this book could not have been written.

September 1997

# Author's note

In this book I have tried to be sensitive to inclusive language and equal opportunities issues. I have used the term 'patient' because it is the most usual way for analysts and psychotherapists to speak of those who are our clients or customers. Similarly, I have used the term 'practitioner' to include all those who practise as analysts, psychotherapists or counsellors.

When listing individuals or organizations I have used alphabetical order unless a hierarchy is intended.

The case material in this book is entirely fictitious, though it draws on my long experience in the field. Any resemblance in any detail to real persons is entirely unintentional.

# Foreword

The huge expansion in the fields of psychotherapy, counselling and analysis has placed questions of ethical codes and practices far higher up everyone's agenda than was the case ten years ago. However, for the most part, discussions of these issues have tended to polarize so that they take place at one extreme of a spectrum or the other.

On the one hand, there are high-level, somewhat abstract, philosophically sophisticated discussions of what exactly constitutes an ethic suitable for psychotherapy work in general. These discussions often cover the extent of the practitioner's responsibilities to the client or patient and do so in terms of the rather specific nature of therapy work which is so often not what it seems: not advice-giving (yet not devoid of advice and influencing), not a rigidly hierarchical relationship (yet not devoid of power issues), not conducted by one who knows, as opposed to one who is supposed to know (yet requiring extensive training on the part of its practitioners).

On the other hand, there are legalistic codes of practice in existence with carefully thought-out procedures balancing the needs of client, practitioner and public. The problem here is that, as consensus on almost any aspect of therapy work is difficult to achieve, the codes of ethics cannot possibly cover every eventuality. They can often seem cut off from the emotional liveliness of the actual work, and be difficult to understand and off-putting to prospective complainants.

It would be both banal and not strictly true to assert that this book steers a magnificently middle course between philosophy and philosophizing on the one hand and codifying and legalism on the other. I think that one huge benefit of Fiona Palmer Barnes' entire approach is that she has chosen to situate her discussion exactly where it should be placed according to the present-day ecology of the psychotherapy and counselling world. Throughout her book we find careful attention being paid to what is actually going on in the ethics area on the ground so that the various classifications she makes and thought-provoking issues she raises are not being imposed on the field but arise out of it. In this sense her book is not only about therapeutic work; it stands as a piece of therapeutic work in itself, given that, in therapy, we try to bring out hidden potentials from what is already there (and often despised because of that) rather than impose something from above.

Continuing to push the ecological metaphor, another observation that I'd like to make concerns the way in which Fiona Palmer Barnes pays sensitive attention to the social and cultural interfaces between therapeutic work and the world of 'the real' in which the work is embedded. In this sense, she may be seen as preparing the ground for the day when British society generally embraces psychotherapy and counselling as part of the landscape, something so ordinary and workaday that many of the extreme positions, for and against, that get taken up these days will come to seem quite ridiculous.

Books like these stand or fall by their utility. It is absolutely clear that this is a supremely useful book. But will it be used? And where? And by whom? The book itself faces the professions of psychotherapy and counselling with an ethical problem. Time and space need to be created for the crucial issues outlined and engaged with herein to be assimilated by the profession as a whole – not just the bureaucrats that it is, inevitably, spawning. Seminars and workshops that make central use of the book will have to come into being and maybe these should not just be offered to trainees and students but to qualified practitioners as well.

Most populist critiques of psychotherapy focus on three things: it doesn't work, it's done by charlatans, and there are as many schools of therapy as there are therapists. Well, without an ethical framework, all the very encouraging research-based evidence that psychotherapy benefits a high proportion of those who experience it will lead to nothing. Without an ethical framework, limiting the impact of charlatans and miscreants will falter. Without an ethical framework with which practitioners of all schools can broadly agree, the tendency in the therapy world to split and split again will continue unchecked. Could a deep and informed discussion of the ethical dimension provide the psychologically unifying factor that the professions themselves so conspicuously lack? If so, then the contents of this book will operate in a healing way, not only at the boundary between the world of therapeutic work and society at large but also in relation to the various cracks and fissures within that world.

Andrew Samuels

Professor of Analytical Psychology, University of Essex

August 1997

# Introduction

There is currently a growing interest in self-regulation and public accountability of the professions in general, and the fields of psychotherapy and counselling have come under particular scrutiny. Concerns about ethical issues are surfacing more and more in the public sphere as the press takes up, and frequently distorts, stories which have clear professional ethical implications. Behind these stories lies the sense that members of the general public expect to complain if they have not been treated with proper respect. This general mood was encouraged and reflected in Britain in recent times by the Conservative government's promotion of citizens' charters.

Against this background of public attention, psychotherapists and counsellors as well as healthcare professionals and people who work with alternative therapies find that the focus is often on them. They also find that they share many similar ethical concerns.

This book is written for all those interested in issues of ethics, codes of practice and ways of dealing with complaints – questions of standards that all of these professional groups face. Its particular orientation comes from the professional practice of its author and it is therefore written mainly with British psychotherapists and counsellors in mind. Much of what it contains, however, will be of interest to the wider audience of care professionals and alternative therapists who share a growing concern about professional complaints and how they are to be managed.

We may wonder why there is such an interest in ethical issues today. These matters used to be the province of the Church; with the introduction of the National Health Service in 1948 the sense of ethical responsibility passed at least in part to the medical professions and the State. It could be said that at that time there was a paternal transference to the medical profession and the State and that the sense that the medical practitioner knew what was best was unquestioned. Much of what has happened since then in society with the growth of individual autonomy has caused more people to question who does know what is best, and the sense has grown of 'Do I not have a say also?' Now that people have to look back two generations or so to find a direct connection with a moral basis or faith in religion, there is a feeling of a moral and religious void. The new debating spaces that are being found for the deep public concern about these issues are mostly in and through the media.

The management of complaints is, on the other hand, seen as an essential expression of dissatisfaction by those who feel, as purchasers of services, that they have not received what they expected. This growing concern of the client group is reflected in the fears of practitioners about how a complaint might affect them. This is a real and potent concern. Experience shows that complaints have not in fact increased dramatically in number. However, there are more cases and they have become far more complicated to deal with.

Concern about how to manage complaints has in its turn led to a tightening up of ethical standards and guidelines for codes of conduct. The clarification of these codes and boundaries is in itself very helpful in the processing of complaints. A proper understanding of ethical issues and careful managing of complaints are also seen as essential factors in maintaining standards and establishing good practice within a profession.

This book is written in the hope of allaying fears. It draws on the author's experience of managing seventy or so complaints from individuals against members or organizations from within the British Association for Counselling and the United Kingdom Council for Psychotherapy.

In the past, the world of alternative therapies has for the most part been viewed from the outside as a secret garden, hidden from most people's eyes, full of wonderful things and hard to find ways into. Practitioners have, on the whole, reinforced this view, perhaps mainly from a fear of not having their work understood and therefore not wanting it to be seen. For those who entered psychotherapy and counselling there was the sense of entering a mystical world which was also quite risky. It could help you and, if you were very fortunate, you might be asked to join it. For those who trained there was a strong sense of entering a novitiate, going through an extended period of training with many hurdles and then going through some initiation ceremony at qualification. Many trainings prided themselves on their standards and the quality of their trainees and graduate therapists. There was a sense that psychotherapists and counsellors knew what the work was about: they understood the 'ethos'.

It is now different. During the last fifteen years, with the proliferation of courses in skills and practice for both counselling and psychotherapy, the sense of mystery has largely disappeared. Many would feel that this is a very good thing. However, what have emerged are difficulties involving ethics, ethos and the attitude of practitioners to the work.

In order to explain the background to these problems it may be useful to set out a brief overview of the profession, looking first at the history of psychotherapy and counselling in the United Kingdom; then at the implications of being a professional person in terms of an awareness of the spirit of the times and the public interest in accountability; and finally, at the need for codes of ethics and practice as statements of good intention, and complaints procedures as providing transparent processes for dealing with complaints.

## A HISTORY OF PSYCHOTHERAPY AND COUNSELLING

The regulation of 'therapeutic activities' started with the medical profession. The profession began to regulate itself in the middle of the nineteenth century; since 1858 there have been a number of Acts of Parliament prescribing its activities. However, it was only after the Second World War that, with the formation of the National Health Service, the State became the main source of all healthcare provision.

The professions supplementary to medicine, such as physiotherapy and radiography, were regulated as late as 1960 by Act of Parliament; but psychotherapy was not included despite considerable lobbying at the time. The medical members of the psychotherapy and, in particular, analytic associations felt that there were potential confusions for them in registration as a profession supplementary to medicine when many of them were already covered by their medical qualifications. Since no universal solution could be found, a large lay psychotherapy group was left out and was not registered under the Act. This decision has profoundly affected the course of the history of analysis and psychotherapy in the UK and thus counselling also. As a result we have the tradition of non-medically qualified analysts and psychotherapists in the UK.

Practitioners of psychotherapy and counselling now frequently work alongside medical practitioners and nursing staff in clinics and hospitals. However, the failure to be included as a profession supplementary to medicine has helped a hierarchy, in terms of training organizations, to

become fixed and has limited the work available to many psychotherapists. This is covertly understood within the profession and
becomes quite evident in the jobs that therapists are appointed to. On the
whole, psychotherapists and those who are analytically trained, particularly those with strong links to the groups with high numbers of
medically qualified practitioners like the British Psycho-Analytical
Society and the Tavistock Clinic, work in NHS hospitals and Child
Guidance clinics. This situation is being challenged and certain
psychiatrists, such as Jeremy Holmes in the West Country, are building
teams drawn from a far broader basis of therapeutic models. Such teams
are rare, and national recognition of psychotherapy or counselling is in
no way formalized.

The only exception is the Association of Child Psychotherapists
which has become recognized by the Department of Health as the body
which performs a particular therapeutic task and which accredits UK
training in child and adolescent psychotherapy.

There are four main bodies that make up the psychotherapy and
counselling establishment in the United Kingdom: the British Psychological Society (BPS), the United Kingdom Council for Psychotherapy
(UKCP), the British Confederation of Psychotherapists (BCP) and the
British Association for Counselling (BAC).

The British Psychological Society was founded in 1901, incorporated
by Royal Charter in 1965 and has maintained a register of members
since 1987. Of its 13,000 members 8,000 are Chartered Psychologists.
Chartered Psychologists have a degree in psychology and are particularly concerned with scientific data and research. The BPS recognizes
courses in educational psychology and clinical psychology and some of
the latter have a considerable specialism in psychotherapy. The BPS is
now accrediting counselling psychology courses.

The United Kingdom Council for Psychotherapy is an umbrella
group of organizations working in a psychotherapeutic manner. The
members are grouped into sections according to their orientation. For
example there are sections for analytical psychology and for humanistic
practitioners. The 'therapies' practised by its member organizations
range from analytical psychology to Gestalt and from psychoanalytic
psychotherapy to cognitive therapy.

Historically the traditions represented by the UKCP arose in a number
of ways: first out of the analytic tradition and the influence of the
Tavistock Clinic, with the work that was done during the Second World
War on the psychological functioning of soldiers, prisoners of war
and those who suffered by the actions of armies of occupation; second

out of the work of the child developmental theorists; and lastly out of influences from the United States.

The Council itself arose out of government pressure in the early 1980s for the practice and profession of psychotherapy to be regulated. In 1982 the British Association for Counselling organized a symposium in Rugby to discuss the issues raised by the Foster Report, 'Enquiry into the Practice and Effects of Scientology' and the Siegert Report, 'The Professions' Joint Working Party on Statutory Registration of Psychotherapists'. This became known as the Rugby Conference. The Rugby Conference was transmuted in 1989 into the United Kingdom Standing Conference for Psychotherapy and in 1992 into the UKCP. The UKCP embraces many traditions of psychotherapy, and its member organizations reflect the growing interest in personal autonomy and the value of the psychological therapies in helping individuals in times of distress. The UKCP's policy is to establish psychotherapy as a post-graduate profession. It publishes a national register of the members of its constituent organizations.

The British Confederation of Psychotherapists represents the most orthodox tradition and includes among its member organizations the Institute of Psychoanalysis, the training organization of the British Psycho-Analytic Society, and those trained at the Tavistock Clinic. Most members of these organizations are lay practitioners. The existence of the lay practitioner is peculiar to the United Kingdom and arose out of the decision of the Institute of Psychoanalysis, in the 1930s, to train lay analysts. The analytical world has always kept itself aloof, seeing its long training requirements and demanding academic pre-qualifications as evidence of greater specialism. It has suffered its own splits and schisms: the Jungian world in particular now consists of four separate groups, while the Freudians hold themselves together as one organization with three training streams.

The British Psycho-Analytic Society and the Tavistock Clinic and its many trainings have spawned further organizations. All of these make up the backbone of the British Confederation of Psychotherapy, a group that split from the United Kingdom Council for Psychotherapy in 1992.

Counselling has developed in the United Kingdom since the 1950s. An important impetus came from both the established and nonconformist churches, where clergy with progressive views felt the need to incorporate into their work a greater understanding of the new psychological theories, particularly those deriving from post-war work in child development, and the new understanding of the effects of attachment, separation and loss in bereavement. Some clergy attended clinical pastoral education courses in the United States and brought back to the United Kingdom the patterns of training and training therapy associated with these courses. Other strands in the counselling tradition also came from the United States in the 1960s, from movements that were trying to simplify and refine the important understandings of psychoanalysis and provide effective treatment on a short-term or less frequent basis than psychotherapy. The British Association for Counselling came into existence as a combining of many of these interest groups and those who were working as counsellors in universities, education and industry. More recently a smaller group has developed in Scotland called the Confederation of Scottish Counselling Agencies (COSCA).

Of these four main bodies, then, two are membership organizations, the BPS and the BAC, and two are umbrella organizations, the BCP and the UKCP. Three of them are registering bodies, the BPS, the UKCP and the BCP, while the BAC is a learned society which has recently produced a registration system for qualified and accredited members. The BAC, the UKCP and the BCP have organizational members who have autonomy over their own affairs as long as they do not infringe the codes of ethics and practice or guidelines of the umbrella organization to which they belong.

The BPS has a generic code of conduct for all its members. It has its own Counselling Psychology Division which produces professional practice guidelines and guidance on good practice. Standards are monitored and complaints are managed centrally.

The UKCP aims to improve standards in the field: it provides guidelines for codes of ethics and practice and for complaints procedures, and it monitors standards. It expects its member organizations to set and maintain their own standards, have ethical codes and manage their own complaints; but there is a clear appeals procedure to the central UKCP registration board.

The BCP is different in that, although it is active in promoting the interests of its member organizations and providing a register of the member organizations, ethical matters are left entirely to those member organizations. The BCP does monitor the standards of the member organizations; however there is no mechanism for complaints or appeals to the central administration.

The BAC is open not only to practitioners but anyone interested in counselling. It has its own codes of ethics and practice, and a complaints procedure, with which all members are required to comply. The BAC is concerned with professionalism and the standing of counsellors in society, as well as with determining standards and accreditation procedures. The BAC encourages member organizations to deal with their own complaints. If, however, the complainant feels that the matter has not been dealt with adequately, the BAC will hear the complaint centrally.

The BPS and the BAC, because they hear complaints centrally, have the greatest experience of managing complaints. They have also been involved in supporting members at Race Relations Tribunals and Industrial Tribunals.

It is necessary to appreciate the differing nature and complexity of these structures in order to understand how the umbrella organizations and member organizations manage their professional members, maintain standards and address ethical issues and complaints.

## PROFESSIONALISM AND ACCOUNTABILITY

If we call ourselves professionals and say that we belong to professional organizations, what do we mean by these statements? A professional organization represents a discrete group of people performing a particular task to a particular standard. For psychotherapy and counselling the task would be seen in terms of helping the client to understand their own inner world, their mental functioning and its limitations, in such a way that they may understand their own decision-making and feel that they have some sense of choice in doing so.

The formation of groups of professional practitioners has been a gradual process and unusual in a number of ways. Training has taken place in privately run associations, schools and colleges, each with its own fiercely protected ethos. The suggestion of combining into organizations like the UKCP, and to some extent the BCP, was seen by many as threatening their individual identity and independence.

Although it went against the ethos of such organizations, they have been obliged to combine in order to survive in an increasingly regulated world. The demand for public accountability has caused the profession to embark on self-regulation. Regulation has not been imposed from outside.

Psychotherapy and counselling are now more popular than ever. Members of the profession have successfully promoted them; and there is an ever-growing demand for therapy and for courses, as well as a greater willingness by the public to consult psychotherapists and counsellors. Many thousands of people who have attended courses in counselling skills or listening skills now have some insight, however limited, into the ways that psychotherapeutic work is done. Through the greater use of helplines and the growth in counselling after national disasters the profile of counselling has been raised. Marital therapy has become acceptable, and there is a growing sense that couples can use such services to attend to the welfare of their marriages as well as at times of marital breakdown.

With the popularizing of the therapies and their greater use also comes criticism. This can be seen as a healthy challenge to a still largely unregulated profession or as persecution of a group of well-meaning, hard-working therapists by the broadsheet press. Some practitioners resent this attention in the press since they see their work as highly accountable through supervision or consultation. Others, dealing with patients who have been casualties of the bad practice of a previous therapist, may feel that registration and regulation are a necessary part of professional development and a necessary protection of professional reputation. Whatever one's view, such criticism causes the profession to be on its toes and practitioners to examine their therapeutic practice.

## CODES OF ETHICS AND PRACTICE

Codes of ethics and practice are reflections of appropriate standards of behaviour, of professional judgement and integrity. It is on such ideals that the confidentiality which is the foundation of trust between practitioner and patient can be based. The purpose of the codes is to give clarity to what is acceptable practice and what is not. If an organization possesses the awesome power to remove a practitioner from its register, with all the consequences that will have on his or her life and livelihood, it should feel a compulsion to provide for that person a template against which to measure his or her conduct and practice. Similarly the hearing of complaints needs to be managed carefully and well since these are disciplinary tribunals, not courts of competent jurisdiction. However, the practitioner, like any other who is subject to the processes of a professional body, faces a double jeopardy: a professional disciplinary hearing and the possibility of the complainant pursuing the matter in a court of law.

Ethics are not legally enforceable, they are only morally binding. Codes of ethics and practice and complaints procedures have not as yet been tested at Judicial Review. In order to fulfil public expectation and the general demand for accountability, complaints procedures are necessary and codes of ethics and practice give a structure against which complaints may be heard. The writing and implementing of a code also offers the possibility of regularizing practice and raising its standards. Certainly there has been a general tightening up and raising of standards taking place resulting from the moves towards national registers by all four organizations, the BAC, the BCP, the BPS and the UKCP.

We have seen how the psychotherapy and counselling professions have developed over the past half century out of many diverse roots, and how today they form a complex network with varying and sometimes conflicting philosophies. This diversity makes the task of self-regulation particularly important, and particularly difficult. The role of codes of ethics and complaints procedures is of the greatest significance in establishing and maintaining public confidence in the profession.

# Chapter 1

# Purpose, ethics and ethos

In this chapter we look at the purpose of therapeutic activity and consider what its underlying values are. We also look at the different types of organization within the profession and the different pressures they give rise to in the management of good practice.

In recent consultations, the purposes of therapeutic activity were defined by practitioners as follows:

1  to provide a service within an ethical and theoretical framework;
2  to provide an appropriate environment in which to assist patients to identify, clarify and explore their difficulties;
3  to offer a therapeutic relationship which aims to facilitate increased self-understanding;
4  to help patients to gain a greater understanding of both current and past experiences and feelings.

The therapeutic process can involve one or more of the following objectives:

- to alleviate conflict, distress and mental suffering;
- to enhance self-esteem and self-acceptance;
- to increase personal effectiveness;
- to expand the capacity to develop positive relationships with others;
- to explore alternatives and make choices;
- to act with greater spontaneity and autonomy;
- to bring about continuing change, growth and self-development;
- to enjoy a better quality of living;
- to tolerate states of unhappiness.[1]

---

[1]  Bell, D. and Innes, S. (1996) *Interim Report*, Advice Guidance Counselling and Psychotherapy Lead Body, DFEE.

These objectives may be familiar to many practitioners but we rarely articulate them. Some will recognize the list as describing exactly what they do in their therapeutic work. However others, such as psycho-dynamic psychotherapists or analytical psychologists, may feel that such objectives refer too much to the outer world and do not truly reflect the work being undertaken between themselves and their patients, which can often result in considerable inner understanding and change with little apparent external effect. These more internal objectives are also important.

If we examine the values behind our work, we might say that they are determined by *ethics* and *ethos*. The ethos of our practice may depend on our particular therapeutic orientation or on the organization which trained us; and we shall consider this shortly. Let us first look at the question of ethics.

*Ethics* is about universal principles, but it may also be defined as 'a code of behaviour considered correct, especially that of a particular profession'.[2] As psychotherapists, we would probably all accept that the following four principles are fundamental to our work:

1  the principle of maximizing benefit and minimizing harm;
2  the principle of achieving the greatest good;
3  the principle of acting justly;
4  the principle of respecting autonomy.

Let us look at each of these concepts in turn. First, how can we maximize benefit and minimize harm to patients or, alternatively, to candidates in training? In the case of patients, we try to help them gain greater inner and outer understanding of themselves. This will lead to a fuller understanding of their actions and an increased sense of individuality and autonomy, enabling them to take more control over their own lives. In the case of candidates, we try to give them the best training possible so that they become competent practitioners and gain the greatest possible insight into that role.

The principle of minimizing harm is profoundly important. Harm may be done to a patient, for example, in a case where a practitioner says something in an early session that, though it might be an apt inter-pretation, could destabilize the patient. How often have we heard in a supervision or consultation: 'I went to see Mr Jones and he told me I

---

[2]  *Collins Dictionary* (1979) London and Glasgow: Collins.

should just leave home.' It is unlikely that Mr Jones said any such thing. He may have confronted the patient in a particular way. But what is important is what the patient heard; and in this case he *heard* a permission or a challenge to take an action that may have proved irreversible. It is important that the practitioner should bear in mind a responsibility for 'the greater good'; for the family or society. In this case he or she needed to encourage the patient to take time to reflect and consider the implications of what he was feeling and doing.

Second, how can we achieve the greatest good? For some patients this implies discovering their limitations and potential, while for others it might involve understanding their own needs or desire for independence. Again, the greatest good may have far more to do with the wider context of family or society, rather than just the individual.

Third is the principle of acting justly. Justice is about acting in a fair and balanced way. In therapeutic work this is complicated by the fact that practitioners are working with their patients at both a conscious and an unconscious level. It is important for each of us to consider whether we do act justly with each of our patients. If we see that we are not doing so, we often realize that we are caught in some unconscious process or some sado-masochistic mechanism. It is important to bring anything of this nature into the work with the patient as soon as possible, as it may otherwise undermine the therapy. It should also be brought into supervision so that the practitioner can understand his or her own part in it. Working through such a problem is in itself therapeutic.

Fourth, is the principle of respecting autonomy. Autonomy may be defined as the right of every individual to determine their own actions and to express themselves in whatever way they may choose. Therapists are often seen by those outside the profession as masters of manipulation. This impression may be given because we work in a lateral or indirect way: we listen for clues to unconscious processes and then apply theoretical principles to what we are hearing. The practitioner needs to be sure that he or she is respecting the patient's autonomy and not using theoretical arguments to keep the patient feeling powerless.

Ethical principles are the informing elements of codes of ethics and practice or guidelines for ethical practice. They may be written in a number of ways. Some codes, like those of many UKCP organizations, do not separate ethics from practice, while the BAC and others do.

A code of ethics outlines the fundamental values and principles that underlie the therapeutic work, whereas the practice element of the code applies these ethical principles to the work. Codes of ethics and practice normally include the following elements:

- a statement about the therapeutic model;
- what a competent practitioner in that model should be;

followed by sections which cover the practitioner's:

- responsibilities to the patient;
- responsibilities for himself or herself;
- responsibilities to colleagues.

These will be discussed in some detail in Chapter 3.

*Ethos* is defined in the Collins Dictionary as 'the distinctive character, spirit and attitudes' of an organization. The ethos surrounding our work, and the values we bring to it, often stem originally, as has been said, from the founders of our particular therapeutic school. Until recently there has seemed little reason to question these values: we accepted them simply as part of our training. However, new regulation now requires them to be clearly defined and to be translated into codes of practice so that standards can be set and monitored.

Let us look at the different types of organizations and the variety of psychotherapeutic and counselling services they offer. They include agencies that provide services to the public, organizations that train practitioners, and professional organizations to which practitioners belong. Because there were no models for these organizations to follow at their inception, they have often developed structures that reflect the idiosyncrasies and philosophies of their founders. These enclosed structures in turn often affect the way ethical matters are viewed and how the management of complaints is dealt with.

Therapeutic institutions generally conform to one of three types, each representing a particular orientation and each presenting particular difficulties when complaints arise. The three types are: those whose structure reflects their therapeutic theories; those that were founded by a group of friends or colleagues; and those that were formed in reaction to another organization.

The first kind of organization is one whose structure is seen as the outward manifestation of its values and ethos. We might call this the *therapeutic model* type. It includes, for example, some psychodynamic groups as well as some of the more avant-garde groups that originated in the United States. When they began to organize themselves to train new therapists they wanted their organizations to reflect their therapeutic approach. For example, psychoanalytically orientated groups created highly defined structures, reflecting the highly defined operating structure of the therapeutic work of an analyst or psychoanalytically orientated psychotherapist; while another organization, training group therapists, might reflect their own ethos in incorporating ideas such as having staff group time in which to reflect on the workings of the team. Other organizations might have mirrored in their structures the weak boundaries and unclear responsibilities of their clinical work; in time these organizations become completely unmanageable.

Second, there are organizations that were founded by a group of friends or colleagues. We can call these the *collegiate* type. Their organizational structure was created to suit particular individuals with their own strengths and weaknesses and these structures became fixed. Since the founders were often very strong personalities the structures would reflect their idiosyncrasies. For the second generation there may be some problems, but they, at least, remember why the structure is as it is. But for the third generation there can be greater difficulties because the original history of the organization has become mythic and the memory of how matters were dealt with has been lost. Within such organizations individuals may find themselves being asked to play a role they never offered to play, and expected to act in the style of the previous occupant of that role.

Third, there are the organizations that were formed in reaction to other organizations. We can call this the *reactive* type. They may set up structures containing many rebellious or defensive devices, which may prove to be limiting and inflexible. Such organizations can be very hard to manage; some can be anarchic.

Each of these types of institution will reflect the needs and desires of their founders in the structures they have adopted. Structures are needed to get the organizations going. However, the structures that are thus formed may be arbitrary, and are rarely orthodox. This in itself could be a strength at first, but it may give rise to future difficulties, as the structures may not be adaptable or sustainable when it comes to future generations.

A further complication may be added if the founders were close friends, or even sexual partners. In these cases the cross-over between formal roles and friendship or partnership adds to the muddle and boundaries become confused. So often it is just this kind of confusion that leads to complaint.

Particular kinds of problems may arise in each of the types of organization. Let us look firstly at the therapeutic model type. We could see the structuring of many psychoanalytically orientated organizations as being a reflection of the model of work they do. They normally have an ordered hierarchical structure which includes professional committees, training committees and scientific meetings. The ordered nature of the fifty-minute session with prescribed times and days of the week is reflected in the structure, as is the way in which a candidate qualifies, or a practitioner becomes a supervising or training analyst. These small, enclosed organizations can experience particular difficulties in managing complaints because everyone knows everyone. Older members will often have had more recent graduates either in analysis or supervision with them, and this can make it hard to find truly independent people to hear complaints.

Second, let us look at a specific example of the collegiate type of organization. It was founded and run by two people who were partners, Joyce and Joan, and another colleague, John, who had trained with Joan. As with many therapeutic associations, the threesome believed that they had something particular and special to offer. Because of this they felt it was important that all their potential candidates, actual candidates and supervisees should be in therapy and supervision with them. These three were also on all assessment committees, along with two other colleagues who helped to run the training courses. The difficulties of keeping boundaries of confidentiality between therapy, supervision and assessment were most complex, and since the staff members all trusted one another, these boundaries were often broken.

The trainees soon felt the effects, because it became clear that, for example, information given in therapy was known elsewhere. In cases when this was felt to be to the student's benefit it was perceived as the 'parents' caring and knowing. However when a student's progress was questioned and it was suggested that he needed more therapy and longer in training, he challenged the assessment committee and eventually a complaint was made.

This example demonstrates the need for clear boundaries to be kept between the professional roles that an individual plays and any personal friendships and partnerships. This may seem to be obvious, but such confusions arise all too often in many organizations.

The third example concerns a placement agency which could be seen as an organization of the reactive type. In a placement agency candidates see patients under supervision in order to gain experience. A candidate, Annie, was sent to work with a bereavement service whose management structure, created in reaction to previous experience of the co-ordinators of the agency, happened to be completely open and democratic, with past patients represented on the management group. Problems arose because Annie's outlook did not accord with this. She came from an organization that had a strict hierarchy and she had little respect for the democratic approach. She felt that it led to disorganization and that consultation took up too much of her time. She took on various tasks, made herself invaluable to the organization and thus went all out to accrue power so that she could impose her own working style on the organization. The reactive style of the agency caused a lack of clear leadership in the organizational structure, so that it took the united action of the whole staff and management group to raise a grievance and act to re-establish a structure that the majority of the workers in the agency supported.

Psychotherapists and counsellors may have many different purposes or priorities in their work. But all subscribe to certain universal ethical principles. Being mindful of these principles, and bearing in mind, as well, the way in which their approach to the work may be shaped by the ethos of their school, will assist not only in dealing justly with patients but also in understanding and handling situations that might otherwise lead to complaint.

# Chapter 2

# Competence

Professional competence implies a standard of practice that in Winnicott's terms is 'good enough'.[1] Others might refer to this as 'good practice' or a level of practice which other practitioners would recognize as acceptable. In this chapter we will look at competence or good practice in terms of:

- individual practice;
- training;
- placements;
- supervision;
- organizational competence;
- the trainer or supervisor;
- employment.

There are three important aspects to the idea of good practice, each of which evolves as the concept becomes recognized within a profession. First, it reflects a consensus concerning the standard of work of a 'reasonably competent' practitioner, who would be acceptable to the majority of practitioners within the profession; it also reflects the legal standard which would be expected by the courts in a negligence action (the defence would quote the the 'Bolam principle' where a substantial body of reputable practitioners support the defendant's method of treatment). Second, it provides a standard or benchmark against which all practice within the profession can be measured. Third, individual practitioners can be required to reach this standard in order to attain a professional status, and may then be held accountable for their clinical practice.

---

[1] Winnicott, D. (1960) 'Ego Distortion in Terms of True and False Self', in *The Maturational Processes and the Facilitating Environment*, London: Hogarth.

## INDIVIDUAL PRACTICE

Individuals become competent practitioners in psychotherapy and counselling through a variety of experiences, but there are three significant elements: training; practice; and personal experience of analysis, psychotherapy or counselling.

Training is an increasingly important element in becoming a practitioner. As professionalism develops, so do the formality and requirements of the training and the additional experiences which are considered helpful, such as a psychiatric hospital placement or child observation. This increasing formality also aids moves towards statutory regulation.

The second element, universal to all practitioners, is the experience of working with patients under close clinical supervision. This may happen in a variety of settings.

The third element, personal experience of psychotherapy, is not universal. Psychotherapy and analytic organizations consider personal experience to be a vital part of training and expect considerable analytic work to have taken place before training begins. During psychotherapy training the candidate would work with an analyst or psychotherapist who is an approved 'training therapist'. Analytic associations expect candidates to work with training analysts from within their own organizations and this is approved of as standard practice.

The requirements of counselling courses, on the other hand, vary considerably. Some organizations expect the candidate to have personal experience of psychotherapy or working with an experienced practitioner whose training and orientation is compatible with the course. Others require the candidate simply to work in a 'therapeutic manner', experiencing counselling from a senior student from the same training organization.

## TRAINING

In recent years there has been a rapid growth at all levels in the numbers of training courses available in counselling and psychotherapy. Some may involve very little initial assessment of suitability for those enrolling. For example many professionals from associated fields, such as nursing, medicine and education, may take courses to improve their counselling skills, to assist in the performance of their primary role. Clearly they will not be aiming to provide the same kind of service as that offered by a professional psychotherapist or counsellor, and these courses therefore do not involve a rigorous assessment process. There are also counselling courses which, for reasons of equal opportunities policies, accept all candidates.

The more intensive the course the more complex the assessment process. The assessment for courses registered with the BAC, the BCP, the BPS or the UKCP is managed in a more formal way; most involve detailed application forms, interviews and references.

The key question that will be considered at interview by a course organizer is whether the applicant is likely to make enough progress to reach a sufficient standard to pass and, therefore, to be fit to practise. There is an ethical issue here. The course providers need to be confident that most accepted candidates will reach the required standard and that when they graduate they will practise in a competent and ethical way. It is the task of the training organization to assist candidates to the satisfactory completion of training or to warn them during their course of study if they are not, or may not be, considered suitable to qualify at the end. Likewise it is important to the candidates that, if they are accepted in good faith on a course, they may expect, all things being equal, that they will complete it satisfactorily and become competent practitioners.

Candidates must be fully informed at the outset about all financial commitments. They must be given details of fees, and any additional financial requirements such as residential weekends, seminars, supervision costs and therapy costs.

The question of competence of trainers is one that has been addressed over the past few years by the British Association for Counselling (BAC), the British Confederation of Psychotherapists (BCP), the British Psychological Society (BPS) and the United Kingdom Council for Psychotherapy (UKCP). Each of them now monitors and thus accredits its own training courses.

Traditionally the education of psychotherapists has been seen to be the task solely of experienced practitioners. Of course this can be questioned, but it is important to remember that it is the knitting together of experience and practice that is key to the training of psychotherapists. Training must constantly refer to practice, and the competence to practise can only be assessed by other practitioners. Regrettably, academic institutions are now increasingly using non-practitioners to teach psychotherapy and counselling courses. The element of passing on a good and an appropriate model to trainees is a key issue since it is central to the competent functioning of the trainee.

## PLACEMENTS

Many courses simply consist of theory and role-play, and require the trainees to arrange their own placements with a counselling agency. Many low-cost agencies, in their turn, rely on such trainees in order to maintain their services.

Placement agencies normally assess trainees' suitability to work with patients before they start. Inevitably some will be found not to have reached a sufficient standard or to be unsuitable to work with patients. In some cases this will be discovered at assessment, in others it may not be discovered until the candidate has begun to work with patients. This can present the agency with the dilemma of whether the trainee should continue in the placement. For the agency, the patient must be their central concern and inadequate candidates pose a real problem. Sometimes the agency has to terminate a placement because the candidate has been unable to learn from supervision, in order to safeguard patients. As with a training course, the placement agency is adding its imprimatur to the candidate's portfolio of qualifications. The candidate will use this portfolio to complete training or to gain further training or qualification. If the agency continues the placement of an unsatisfactory candidate then it may be not giving the best service possible to patients. It may also tacitly be helping a poor practitioner to qualify.

## SUPERVISION

Supervision of clinical work is a powerfully important element in training and assessment and the supervisor has a considerable responsibility to both patient and trainee. This has been recognized by umbrella organizations, who are increasingly encouraging those who undertake the supervision of others to take on supervisory or consultative support for their supervision work.

Supervision of clinical work normally takes place in one of three ways: individually, with a practitioner who may or may not be independent of the training organization; within the training organization, based on work done with patients in a placement agency; or within the placement agency.

Supervision is about providing a model of good ethical and competent practice. Great care needs to be taken in clarifying all relationships and avoiding dual roles, for example having the same person acting as supervisor and/or trainer, and/or therapist and/or assessor to a candidate. In my experience, confusion in core role-relationships invariably results in confusion in the candidate. Candidates who experience such confusion often fail to question it and replicate this confusion in their own work. Where overlapping roles exist they need to be questioned: what constitutes best ethical practice? What is fairest and least harmful and therefore best for the candidate in terms of the training?

When the supervision is with a senior practitioner who is independent of the candidate's training organization, the boundaries are clear and, apart from the various projections the candidate and the supervisor may have about the training organization, an understanding of how confidentiality is to be maintained, and the roles and responsibilities of both parties are clear.

However, if supervision is with a senior practitioner of the candidate's training organization, this can lead to confusion. For example, if a candidate working in private practice as part of their counselling or psychotherapy training is being supervised by someone who is a member of the training committee of the training organization, this supervisor will certainly be submitting full reports on the candidate at regular intervals to the training organization. There may therefore be a confusion of roles, between that of assessor and supervisor and also between the supervisor's responsibilities to candidate and patient. It is advisable, where possible, to avoid such a situation.

If supervision of work carried out at a placement agency takes place within the training organization, the trainers, although they may have a clear sense of the therapeutic work being done by the candidate, may have little idea of how he or she is performing within the agency in terms of responsibility, team working or administration. It is essential to have good communications and reporting mechanisms between the course trainers and agency staff if this system is to work well.

Many placement agencies prefer their own staff to supervise candidates since the agency then holds clinical responsibility for patients and confidentiality can be maintained within the organization. Thus, the agency, through supervisors' reports, will have a clear understanding of what is happening to the patients that it is responsible for and will have an all-round sense of the candidates' performance and abilities. This is the most satisfactory arrangement for an agency. However the candidate's training organization may feel that it is not sufficiently involved.

Relationships between training organizations and placement agencies are often poor. This has been the cause of many a problem. It is important to have a clear sense of their respective responsibilities. The agency is primarily responsible for the patient; the training organization is

primarily responsible for the candidate. The staff of the training organization and the agency need to communicate with one another efficiently
and effectively in order to serve the needs of both patient and candidate.

## ORGANIZATIONAL COMPETENCE

Training organizations, placement agencies and professional associations alike need to be competent and efficiently managed. In the past
many have not been very efficient, relying, as so many small organizations do, upon individuals willing to do whatever was needed. This
sometimes resulted in misunderstandings. However, over the last decade
most have developed the necessary systems to manage themselves, their
finances and their training courses. Most have also become companies
limited by guarantee and taken on charitable status. These developments
have been important in giving their members, as well as the outside
world, a sense of order and competence. Given the strict requirements of
the umbrella organizations there is now every reason to believe that
proper professional standards have been extended to all training and
professional organizations registered with the BAC, the BCP, the BPS
and the UKCP.

## THE TRAINER OR SUPERVISOR

Professional competence, once achieved, needs to be developed. It might
be seen ideally as 'life-long learning'. Part of a practitioner's professional development may be the experience of working as a trainer and
supervisor. Professional bodies need to consider at what stage graduates
should be allowed to become supervisors and trainers, and new
regulations set out by the BAC, the BPS and the UKCP are now
addressing this question. Within each umbrella organization it is, in any
case, considered essential for anyone applying for trainer or supervisor
accreditation to have considerable experience of practice.

However, the current proliferation of counselling courses of differing
length and content means that individuals can complete a comparatively
basic, academically orientated, course and immediately move on to
further qualification through a supervision course, or become trainers,
without having had any real experience of therapeutic practice.

Until recently there was a clear apprenticeship system operating in
training organizations. When a practitioner was qualified and had gained
some further experience, he or she might be asked to offer a series of
training seminars on a particular subject. The practitioner would be

expected to refer both to literature and to a range of clinical experience. This rather formal system of qualification acknowledges that 'graduate' members have a clear status within the organization. The role of seminar leader is seen as a way of contributing to the life of their professional body, to be followed in due course by preparation and application to be a supervisor or training therapist. At each stage the graduates would be expected to be able to speak with confidence about their philosophy as well as their work with patients. The apprenticeship system offers a clear delay between qualification and working as a supervisor, allowing time to gain wider experience of working with patients. Those who believe in the power of the group to make good decisions might favour this system. However, the traditional system may also have disadvantages in that senior practitioners may become protective of their power and position and not make way for younger members. It is for these reasons that many organizations have worked hard over recent years to devise more democratic systems that recognize the experience of their graduates.

## EMPLOYMENT

How can employers know that the practitioner they are about to employ is competent? Qualified psychotherapists' names are listed in the two national registers published by the BCP and the UKCP. BAC accredited counsellors' names appear in the new *United Kingdom Register of Counsellors*, while the *Counselling and Psychotherapy Resources Directory*, also published by the BAC, lists psychotherapists and counsellors accredited or qualified by the BAC, the BCP, the BPS and the UKCP.

Many job advertisements now ask for applications from BCP/UKCP/ BAC accredited psychotherapists and counsellors. This is a clear way in which employers can know that the competence of practitioners has been scrutinized and their experience reviewed by other competent practitioners.

In order to ensure that they choose a suitable candidate, potential employers might consider getting advice from one or more of the national organizations about what to look for when interviewing a psychotherapist or counsellor, and possibly include someone on the selection panel who knows about the complexity of qualifications in the area. For example, even now there are enormous variations in the quality of courses that might be described as being at 'diploma level'. Some require a commitment of half a day during term time for two years, while others are full time for one year plus one day a week for a further year, working to a far higher academic level. There are also variations in style. One GP practice might favour a psychodynamic counsellor or psychotherapist, while another might want someone from a humanistic tradition.

The fixing of standards by which to judge competence in practice is a vital part of the establishment of the psychotherapy and counselling professions. Until recently it was very difficult for prospective employers, trainees or patients to be sure that any practitioner or training organization they chose would offer them the standard of tuition or therapy they had a right to expect. Now, however, with the increasing level of regulation and the introduction of codes of practice, the public can be confident that any accredited member of the professions is going to be able to provide a competent service.

# Chapter 3

# Contract

Members of the public are increasingly accustomed to making *contracts* with professional people, be they surveyors, architects or the person who comes to service the central heating boiler. They are also increasingly aware of their own contractual rights, as in standards set out in citizens' charters, and have an understanding of what an individual should expect from service providers. Those who work in an institutional setting may have some practical experience of these attitudes. However they may be less familiar to the therapist who is a private practitioner. Increasingly, patients' expectations about the services they receive may not be in line with the way practitioners deliver them.

In the therapeutic profession the word 'contract' is used in a specific sense not precisely identical with the general understanding of the term nor with the legal definition. In the therapeutic context a contract is an agreement between two parties, a trainee and a training organization, a practitioner and a patient, a supervisor and a supervisee, or a practitioner and an employing institution. It is particularly important to explain the nature of the therapeutic contract to patients and those who may not be familiar with our profession.

Traditionally the therapeutic contract has been verbal, as were contracts in business a generation ago or in the professions such as medicine or the law where deals were made by shaking hands. However, increasingly, in business and the professions, contracts are being written down; in the field of counselling also, legal opinion favours this development. In our increasingly litigious society, practitioners can expect that more informal complaints may lead to formal legal claims in the court, with clients seeking financial compensation. There have been few, if any, successful claims to date: the general view has been that the process of therapy cannot easily accommodate legal concepts such as 'negligence', 'injury', 'reasonable foreseeability' and 'causation'.

However it is thought by legal professionals that this will happen in the near future and then the clarification of expectations between the parties by formalizing contracts with clients and keeping fuller records may well assist therapists in defending claims made against them.

Let us consider the different of types contract.

## THE CONTRACT BETWEEN THE TRAINEE AND THE TRAINING ORGANIZATION

Training organizations are becoming increasingly aware of the necessity of making clear contracts with trainees. The organization, in this case, is the provider of the service and the trainee is the purchaser. Training matters form the basis of about one third of formal complaints, and few training organizations have adequate grievance procedures to deal with them openly and adequately.

It has, in the past, sometimes been very hard for training organizations to define what they require of their trainees for qualification. It is important that they should provide trainees with a clear statement about the standards required for each qualification before they begin studying.

Within any training contract is an understanding that the training organization will support trainees in achieving their qualifications. Therefore, if trainers are concerned about trainees during training, they need to make them aware as early as possible about these concerns and what is needed to remedy the situation. It is sometimes very hard, even for a group of colleagues, to be precise about what aspects of a particular trainee's practice need attention; things such as the trainee's attitude to the patient, their ability to work 'in a therapeutic way' or in 'an analytic way' – aspects which will be examined by assessment committees. It can also be very hard for trainees who are in difficulties with their training to see the difficulty they are in. In Jungian terms, they are so often 'in their complex', having difficulties with just the aspect of work with the patient that causes them most difficulty within themselves, psychically their weakest place. They may well disagree with their trainers about what needs to be done, leading to a collision of views and potential complaints.

Difficulties may arise for a trainee when several different contracts overlap. To illustrate this let us look at the problems that Ann experienced. Ann was in training with an institution. She had chosen it because her own therapist, Jill, worked there and Ann felt positive about her. So, before and during training Ann was in a contractual relationship with Jill. By undertaking the training, Ann took on a contractual relationship with the training organization and vice versa. Jill was one of the senior course tutors and an assessor of Ann's training. Jill's partner, Bob, was a co-founder of the institution and became Ann's supervisor. He also sat on the assessment committee. We now have a contract between the institution and Ann; a contract between the institution and Jill; a contract between the institution and Bob; a therapeutic contract between Ann and Jill; a supervisory contract between Ann and Bob; and a partnership, both emotional and professional, between Jill and Bob. The stage is set for a real difficulty.

Ann entered a phase in her therapy that was angry and she was firmly in a negative transference. She fought her therapist and she fought the institution. Jill and Bob, as part of an assessment committee, decided to terminate her training. Ann felt unjustly treated and complained.

Institutional 'incest' of the kind so well illustrated by Ann's case, happens in all kinds of organizations. Many complaints arise out of situations of this kind where roles and boundaries are confused and unclear, and staff members have many roles. Sometimes it happens because the organization is short staffed, the case in institutions which have only been training students for a few years; or sometimes because it is in a geographical area where there are few trained people. In other organizations there is a sense of exclusivity because the ethos of the training is seen to be so special. In a few cases institutional incest can persist for many years. Needless to say, such situations do not reflect best practice.

Another kind of difficulty that trainees have experienced with training institutions, which might be avoided by the use of clear contracts, has been a 'moving of the goal posts'. Suddenly, halfway through their training, trainees are told that they are required to achieve a higher standard, with consequent increased commitments of time and money. They may be required to pay for extra supervision or for additional training weekends. Sometimes these changes have been caused by new regulations for training set out by national umbrella organizations; however, it has not always been clear to trainees whether the changes were primarily for their benefit or for the benefit of the organization.

Contracts between training organizations and trainees are important. A clear statement of what is being offered by the organization, and what is required of the trainees, enables trainees to assess their chances of completing the course successfully. They may otherwise get the impression that they are being kept in training in an unreasonable way and possibly being prevented from qualifying. This can be particularly worrying if the training organization is in financial difficulties and the trainees' fees are its chief source of income.

Disputes over a contract are governed by law and can usually be settled in the Small Claims Court. Claims for negligence due to inadequate contract-making or poor standards may also be dealt with in this way. However, it is generally agreed by the legal profession that issues relating to the content and conduct of the therapeutic work are governed by the regulations, codes of ethics and practice, set down and agreed to by the appropriate professional body, such as the UKCP.

## THE CONTRACT BETWEEN THE PRACTITIONER OR AGENCY OFFERING THERAPY AND THE PATIENT

In private practice a contract for therapy should be negotiated in a session, after some assessment has taken place. It needs to set out an agreed way of working and to define the expectations of both parties. It should cover:

- the kind of therapy being offered;
- the length and frequency of sessions;
- the duration of the treatment;
- the fees to be charged and what happens about missed sessions;
- supervision and limits of confidentiality;
- the code of ethics under which the service is offered.

The agreement should be seen by the practitioner as binding, with the hope and expectation that the patient will treat the contract with equal respect.

Let us look in turn at each of these aspects of the contract with the client.

### The kind of therapy being offered

For the patient, the initial decisions about this will depend on what emerges from the extended assessment period. It also depends on what the patient, or perhaps the patient's partner or family, wishes in terms of commitment both of time and energy, and most importantly what can be hoped for in terms of the depth of the therapeutic work. One person may come on a short-term contract while another may wish to do some very deep work or prepare for analytic training. Whatever the patient and practitioner decide about the potential work they can do together this matter needs to have been discussed and made clear between them.

The practitioner needs to explain the nature of his or her work and its scope, style and what principles inform it; whether it is humanistic, cognitive, integrative or psychoanalytic. It is helpful for the practitioner to say something about his or her qualifications but, in any case, if questions are asked about qualifications they need to be answered; guidelines for codes of ethics and codes of practice require this. It is important that a purchaser of therapeutic services knows as fully as possible what is and what is not being offered.

## The length and frequency of sessions

Some analytic therapists expect sessions up to five times a week. Other practitioners may expect one, two or three regular meetings in a week, and this should be stated, with the times laid out. Some practitioners may meet less frequently but at regular intervals. Others may meet for longer sessions on a less regular basis.

It can be hard for the first-time analytic patient to understand that an analytic hour is not an hour but, in fact, fifty minutes; and this needs to be made clear from the beginning or it may feed concerns that the patient already feels about deprivation or cheating. Patients often find it difficult to understand why the frequency that is being recommended is necessary and an explanation may be required. Once the work is started, the frequency is often felt to be right. Sometimes there is resistance and patients, or their partners, may fear dependency. This can result in sessions being missed, and then charged for. The arrangements about these matters need to be clear and specific from the start.

If the practitioner does not have a waiting room, he or she may need to request at the outset that the patient does not arrive too early. There may also need to be an agreement about contact with the practitioner between sessions, the circumstances when this is acceptable and whether by phone or letter. Whatever the arrangements, they need to be made explicit and the practitioner needs to be sure that the client understands them. Some flexibility may need to be built in. If for example, the patient works on shifts, he or she may have difficulty in attending regular sessions. Then a compromise needs to be reached before the contract is agreed.

## The duration of the treatment

One of the most common questions asked at the beginning of a therapy is, 'How long will it take?' It is one of the hardest questions to answer because the practitioner's experience is that it is likely to take longer than the patient expects. Some psychotherapists and counsellors would see the majority of their work as 'ongoing' or 'open-ended'. In other words, the therapeutic relationship will go on for as long as it is felt by both practitioner and patient that the 'work' will take. Other forms of therapy are short term, for example the five or six sessions that an employee assistance programme will offer. Some practitioners deal with the problem by setting a review date, which acknowledges the patient's concern about time but also allows for the work to continue if needed. Others specify the length of notice that the practitioner would expect from the patient. This equally needs to be made clear to the patient at the outset.

Let us look at the kinds of difficulties a practitioner may experience when the patient does not fully understand the duration of treatment.

Mr Bloom decided to go into therapy with a humanistic practitioner. A series of sessions was arranged at different times each week, since that was the tradition of the practitioner. Each time the block of arranged sessions drew to a close, Mr Bloom missed one or two. His practitioner contacted him, commenting on the missed sessions and suggesting the initial one or two of the next block of sessions. Mr Bloom wanted to continue, in fact the sessions were a lifeline for his own independence from a domineering wife. However, Mrs Bloom asked questions and kept a close tab on things, reading the letters from the practitioner. In the end she was able to manipulate the situation and Mr Bloom stopped his sessions. She then used the thirty to forty letters from his therapist as the basis of the complaint she encouraged Mr Bloom to make against the practitioner on the grounds that he, the patient, had not been encouraged to act in an autonomous way.

We can see how this projection of the fear within the relationship between Mr and Mrs Bloom could become the focus of complaint. However, this complaint was difficult to resolve, partly because it was so close to the difficulties of the couple concerned and so they are unable to see it; but, also, from a purely practical point of view, because the wording of the practitioner's letters was not clear and his words of encouragement were seen by the patient's partner, consciously and unconsciously, as threatening.

Good practice in such a case would have involved the practitioner using greater caution in drawing up the contract and making appointments, and reflecting in the work with the patient and in supervision on the significance of the patient's repeated suggestions that he stop the therapy.

Other difficulties can arise when the patient expects that treatment will be shorter or more immediately effective than it is. After an initial assessment session with a practitioner, Jo, a female patient, was offered short-term therapy. Her condition was considered too acute for long-term work, which might move her into crisis, yet not bad enough for the psychiatric services. Jo did not have this explained and therefore had not understood the reasoning behind the treatment that was being offered to her. However she had some sense of her own fragile state and acted out by making a suicide attempt. Later she complained about the lack of care offered by the agency. A suitable referral to another agency which could have offered either more extensive therapy or greater containment would have been more helpful for Jo.

## The fees to be charged and what happens about missed sessions

All of us who charge fees for the work we do know well that this is one of the key areas where difficulties may arise that express far greater psychological issues than simply the matter of money. It is therefore necessary to be particularly careful about having a contractual agreement which governs fees and states what happens about cancelled sessions, missed sessions and holidays.

The practitioner's usual sessional fee is often inquired about when the first contact is made. The practitioner may have a fixed assessment fee and a variable fee for ongoing work, or the fee may be fixed at the first appointment for that and all subsequent appointments. Whatever the arrangement it needs to be explicit.

Another financial matter that causes particular difficulty is that of paying for every regular session except the conventional breaks taken by the practitioner. Many practitioners take a fortnight off at Christmas and at Easter, and are on holiday for the whole month of August. All arrangements for breaks and holidays by the practitioner need to be made known to the patient well in advance.

If the practitioner expects payment for all the sessions that he or she is available for, and the patient's own holidays fall outside the practitioner's vacation time, the patient will be charge for missed appointments. This convention should be clearly explained at the time of assessment, as otherwise the patient may feel that he or she has been wrongly treated.

Other practitioners, who do not wish to follow such a structured pattern in their work and may wish to be away at other times, need to be particularly clear about what breaks they will be taking, and inform the patient. If a patient chooses to take a holiday at a different time from them, the practitioner may be willing to offer sessions in lieu, or to allow the patient two or three weeks' vacation at a different time from their own. Whatever arrangement is come to, it needs to be seen to be 'fair and reasonable' to both parties. From the practitioner's point of view the time may be reserved for that patient and that patient alone, or he or she may feel able to use a patient's missed session for a particular one-off task and therefore will not need to charge for it. Alternatively practitioners may be totally flexible in how they choose or need to work and be willing to make ad hoc arrangements.

The patient, however, may never be able to take a holiday at the same time as the practitioner, and having to pay for the missed sessions may seem unreasonable. From a contractual point of view it is important to consider whether it is reasonable or not. Ultimately the power lies with the practitioner, and the practitioner needs to recognize this in making a contract that is also fair for the patient.

## Supervision and limits of confidentiality

Supervision, though always a vital part of psychotherapeutic work, was, until the past ten years, rarely spoken of to the patient. Now that the general public has a far greater understanding of the nature of psychotherapeutic work, there is a greater awareness of the need for supervision.

The contract between practitioner and patient needs to explain to the patient that in the course of clinical supervision his or her confidential case material will be shared with the practitioner's supervisor and in some cases the practitioner's agency. This may result in people, who the patient may never meet, knowing a great deal about him or her.

The patient needs to know the limits of confidentiality and the practitioner needs to consider how to communicate this. If they are working in an institution it may be by a statement such as, 'What we say here is confidential to the psychotherapy service.' In private practice the practitioner might say 'What we say here is confidential and remains between us, but from time to time I discuss my work with one or two colleagues and I would expect to be able to discuss our work in this way.

I would, of course, not identify you by name. Is that acceptable to you?' Should the patient wish to know who has access to his or her file, the practitioner, while possibly treating the question as clinical material, needs to inform the patient of the limits of confidentiality.

It is important to explain that supervision is the way that work is monitored professionally and that this serves as a safety net for the patient. If the practitioner expects the patient to respect confidentiality, in the belief that the work needs to be contained within the sessions, this also needs to be agreed in the contract.

## The code of ethics under which the service is offered

The final matter that needs to be mentioned in an initial contract is under which code of ethics the service is offered. The guidelines for codes of ethics and practice of the UKCP, the BCP and the BPS and the codes for counsellors of the BAC make it very clear that practitioners should state to which code they are working and that they will be willing to supply a copy of the code or a complaints procedure if requested. They should also be able to explain and discuss their code with a patient if it is pertinent to do so. (See Appendix 1, p. 116)

## The practitioner's responsibilities to the patient

The practitioner's responsibility to the patient or trainee is paramount. The belief that a patient's or trainee's safety has been put at risk is the most frequently invoked ethical issue in statements of complaint. Patient or trainee safety features in between 80 and 90 per cent of complaints made to the British Association for Counselling. Practitioners may think that they never put patients or trainees at risk, but patients and trainees certainly feel that they do. This includes the potential for or actual physical and psychological harm, and generally means that patients feel themselves to be physically at risk once they have left the consulting room or course session, or psychologically at risk in the sense of 'at risk of breakdown'. This issue is particularly important because many therapeutic orientations might believe that 'breakdown' or a regressed state could well be a part of the work that the practitioner and patient need to do together or that the training organization would consider acceptable for a trainee to go through.

In my experience it is frequently the very vulnerable patient, or his or her partner, who makes a complaint. The partner's role is often an interesting dynamic in itself, having a great deal to do with the power balance within the couple's own relationship that is being threatened by the therapy and the potential for challenge or change that emanates from the work. In other words, in the assessment for ability to work the practitioner needs to have a sense of how vulnerable the patient might really be and gauge the rigidity of the patient's inner world. Without this understanding, problems may arise if active therapeutic work is attempted by a practitioner who cannot offer the experience or depth of work necessary, or where supportive therapy might well be more appropriate. The end result may be a situation where the patient feels his or her safety is at risk and complains.

### The practitioner's responsibilities to himself/herself

This involves the practitioner maintaining their own physical and mental health by observing when they are overloaded and seeing that they are not working for too many hours or beyond their capabilities. Some practitioners run training sessions in the evenings after a heavy day's work. This may work well for some whereas others may find it too taxing and are unable to function properly.

Practitioners are expected to keep their practice within the limits of their own competence. In other words, a practitioner who has been trained as a body therapist should not describe his or her work as psychodynamic simply because he or she has been on a short course on psychodynamic theory, or even because he or she has a supervisor who is psychodynamically trained. These extra workshops should be considered as continuous professional development. Any change in the way a practitioner describes his or her theoretical orientation should stem from significant additional training and qualification in that theoretical model. Similarly, a practitioner in psychoanalytic psychotherapy who has been in therapy or analysis three times a week should not be expected to supervise or practise with supervisees or patients working at four or five times a week. This is what is considered to be good practice and the generally accepted norm of psychoanalytically trained psychotherapists. Though this may sound obvious, complaints are constantly being made against practitioners who are clearly working beyond their competence.

Keeping abreast of current thinking about ethical matters, whether the practitioner agrees with it or not, is important. For instance a trainer, Jasmin, who has held a weekend course at her cottage in Wales for the past fifteen years, finds that her usual helper is unavailable and involves one of her senior trainees as co-leader. The course involves a process group three times a day where both leaders are involved. Annabelle, a group member, believes herself to be the scapegoat of the group and eventually leaves. She then complains about the scapegoating, and questions the trainer's boundaries in holding a training session at her own property, with her trainee as co-leader, and asks for her fees to be returned. Jasmin was continuing to do something she had always done, not realizing that recent professional thinking about boundaries might question the appropriateness of the circumstances.

Another example would happen if a trainer starts a social relationship with a trainee and then finds the trainee complaining when the relationship ends. It is important that the practitioner is not dependent on patients or trainees sexually, socially or financially in any way other than in their clinical or training capacity. Complaints that have been made against the 'elders' in the profession have most often been those which might not have arisen if the practitioner had been in touch with current thinking about boundary issues and practice.

### The practitioner's responsibilities to colleagues

These include being respectful of colleagues' 'reputations' and right to practise and thus, in general, supporting the reputation of the professional association. For a long time it has been considered bad practice knowingly to take on a current patient of a colleague. This could be seen as taking away their trade, but additionally it might be playing into the dynamics being acted out between practitioner and patient. Should the patient be involved in a negative transference to the first practitioner it will not be resolved by changing to another practitioner. The patient may well have moved on to someone else in many previous relationships.

Another responsibility often cited in codes is that the practitioner should not criticize a colleague without first bringing a complaint to the ethics or professional committee, whichever is appropriate, of the organization. The intention is to maintain the good name of the organization. Practitioners are also usually required to report suspected unprofessional conduct by colleagues to their professional organization.

## THE CONTRACT BETWEEN THE SUPERVISOR AND SUPERVISEE

Ongoing supervision is now more often than not a requirement for registration as a psychotherapist or counsellor. It is considered by most orientations to be an essential element of good practice. However, among analytic groups, supervision is only essential during training. The standard of qualification is considered to be at a level where supervision need not be a requirement after qualifying. However, in recent years there has been a growing trend for practitioners to be in some kind of supervisory consultation and this is now generally considered to be good practice.

When two practitioners meet to see if they feel that they can work together they may have the sense that they both already know what goes on in supervision. However the relationship between supervisor and supervisee is complex. The role of supervisor involves being part mentor and part assessor. It is educative in the truest sense, drawing out the best in the supervisee. If the supervisee is fully qualified, then the supervision becomes consultative. Whatever the arrangement is it needs to be acknowledged. In drawing up a contract between supervisor and supervisee they need to consider:

- clinical responsibility;
- insurance cover;
- content and use of time;
- arrangements for crisis management, including access for the practitioner to the supervisor for consultation in a difficulty;
- clarity about codes of ethics the practitioner and supervisor are working to;
- the supervisor's own consultation;
- the fee.

**Clinical responsibility**

If the work is being done for an institution the clinical responsibility for the patient normally rests with the institution. If the practitioner is still in training then clinical responsibility is with the supervisor and training organization, or with the placement agency. Practitioners who are qualified hold clinical responsibility for their own patients.

**Insurance cover**

Both supervisor and practitioner need to be sure that they have adequate insurance cover. This is a requirement in all codes of practice in psychotherapy and counselling. The likely increase in litigation makes this all the more essential. No supervisor should take an uninsured practitioner into supervision or consultation.

## Content and use of time

The supervisor and practitioner need to consider the work that the practitioner wishes to bring to supervision and whether the supervisor agrees that it is appropriate. In the early stages of training the practitioner's entire caseload is usually supervised. Once training is complete the practitioner may wish to concentrate on one patient in supervision. However, in the case of psychotherapy or analytic training the weekly supervision will concern one training patient only. This might be called an 'intensive' model. After training is complete the work in supervision may follow a theme, or it may involve taking an overview of the practice and examining particular troubling issues. This could be called a 'broad brush' model.

The supervisor has to decide if he or she wishes to work in the way the supervisee has suggested. For instance, if a practitioner with a large amount of once-a-week work and one three-times-a-week client wants only to be supervised on the latter, is that appropriate? This decision will be informed by the kind of work that the practitioner has been trained for and the code of ethics he or she is working to. Depending on the size of the practice and nature of the work being done, it may not be appropriate always to use a broad brush model in supervision and never consider any cases in depth. If the practitioner seems to be using crises as a smoke screen so that none of the in-depth work is discussed, a more intensive supervision model might be more appropriate for a time. The supervisor needs to consider whether he or she is getting an adequate view of the work for which he or she is being held responsible.

## Arrangements for crisis management

Crises may happen in any practice and the practitioner and supervisor need to attend to these. Intensive work might then need to be put aside for a session or two. The supervisor and practitioner need to have an agreement about how the practitioner is supported in these circumstances. Most supervisors do not mind practitioners telephoning them within reasonable hours to discuss such a difficulty because such circumstances are rare and usually require a speedy response. However, some supervisors may wish to limit their availability and this needs to be agreed at the outset.

## Clarity about codes of ethics the practitioner and supervisor are working to

The supervisor needs to acquaint him or herself with the code of ethics and practice which the practitioner is working to as well as clarifying the position concerning his or her own code.

## The supervisor's own consultation

The supervisor also needs to give thought to what consultative support will be necessary considering the supervision load he or she is working with. The supervisee needs to know if issues raised in supervision are likely to be discussed elsewhere.

## The fee

See pp. 31–2.

To conclude this section let us look at an example of the kind of difficulty that can arise when there are no clear contracts covering supervision. James was seeing three patients at a placement agency while he was in training. The casework was being supervised in the agency. The agency realized that James was not coming in for his usual sessions. When questioned he said that he had got into a particular difficulty with one patient. He had spoken to Marie, a senior member of his training organization, and she had suggested that he move his patients from the placement agency to the training organization so that she could supervise them herself. Neither the placement agency nor the supervisor at the placement agency had been informed.

Even though there was no formal contract between the supervisor and the supervisee, there were many breaches of the various informal contracts: between James and his patient; James and his supervisor at the placement agency; James and the placement agency; and, the implicit understanding between Marie at the training organization and the placement agency. There were also several breaches of ethical codes.

## THE CONTRACT BETWEEN THE PRACTITIONER AND THE EMPLOYING INSTITUTION

There is a growing concern among practitioners, both within agencies and in private practice, about their relationship with the agencies they work for, such as GP practices, or employee assistance programmes.

Such contracts need close scrutiny. They are effectively three-way contracts between the employer of the counsellor or psychotherapist, the practitioner and the patient. The kinds of question that arise are:

- Who holds clinical responsibility for the patient?
- Who pays for and supervises the work?
- With whom is the patient making the contract: the practitioner, the GP surgery or other agency?
- Is confidentiality held within the agency or between patient and practitioner?

A growing number of doctors, educational establishments and employee assistance services are pressing their employed counsellors for information about their patients and in some cases wanting to connect names with problems, or even have an overview of notes. These requests are usually made in order to justify external funding. There are proven ways in which non-identifiable information can be obtained for statistical purposes. However, if patients and the difficulties they are experiencing can be linked, there may a danger of breaches of confidentiality.

Consider a case, for example, in which a further education estab-lishment pressed its counsellors to inform heads of departments whenever a student was given more than twenty sessions with the college counsellor. An outline of the student's difficulties needed to be given in order to justify further funding. William, who had been depressed since the suicide of a close friend, needed more than twenty sessions. His head of department was told of his depression and its cause, in order to obtain further funding; and thus confidentiality between patient and practitioner was broken.

Such a problem can only be avoided if a clear contract, determining the respective responsibilities of all parties, is drawn up and agreed at the outset.

We have seen in this chapter that clear and binding contracts are essential in every aspect of the psychotherapist's or counsellor's work. They are needed not only to ensure an efficient and visibly fair working relationship between patient, practitioner, supervisor and training organ-ization, but also to help prevent disputes and unjustified complaints. They may in the near future become helpful in defence against legal action.

# Chapter 4

# Confidentiality

Many professionals would say that they offer a confidential service. For instance when you speak to your doctor or your solicitor you would consider it to be in confidence. But what does a confidential relationship between professional and patient or client really mean? What is privileged and what is not?

The concept of confidentiality is central to ethical practice in psychotherapy and counselling. The ethical principles that lie behind confidentiality are those of maximizing benefit, minimizing harm, and of justice and respect for autonomy. These principles apply both to the *practitioner's duty* of confidentiality and the *patient's need* for confidentiality.

The practitioner has a duty to maintain confidentiality in order to deal with sensitive personal information and situations and all the associated intricacies in a contained and professional manner. It provides an aspect of 'the container' in which the therapy takes place. The practitioner will often be dealing with fears, confusions and acting out, and the patient may not understand his or her own responses and reactions. The attitude of the practitioner will be crucial in determining the degree of trust the patient may feel.

The patient has a general and sometimes a specific need to be certain that sensitive personal information will not be passed on to other parties. Without this reassurance, patients will feel inhibited by a lack of safety and they may well leave. The close professional relationship with the practitioner requires openness about the most intimate thoughts, fears and fantasies, current and past situations, opinions and values. All are most vulnerable areas. Trust is needed so that patients can feel sure that their disclosures will not be used to harm them. Or, if they do feel they might, that there is a context in which the work may still continue. Confidentiality may be practised in either an *absolutist* or a *pragmatic* way. The absolutist view, that is that no one but the practitioner should share the patient's confidence, can be very attractive in its simplicity and sureness. But it may well hamper best practice from the client's point of view, as well as interfering with opportunities for negotiation with the patient and limiting choice. It may also severely limit or even prevent the sharing, in a controlled way, of information about practice with colleagues in supervision, consultative support, or case discussion.

The absolutist approach can create difficulties for practitioners, for example when there are obligations to employers or to the law. It can also create difficulties between practitioner, patient and a third party, for example a colleague or a general practitioner. It can foster an atmosphere of secrecy. Practitioners need to be able to manage the complex tensions and differentiate between secrecy and confidentiality.

For example when a patient referred through an employee assistance programme (EAP) arrives in a very distressed mental state, it may be essential to refer the patient speedily through his or her general practitioner to the local psychiatric service. Some communication is often needed with the general practitioner and psychiatrist; communication will certainly be needed with the EAP. However, it may not be necessary to say much. The patient may be able to refer him or herself to the general practitioner, perhaps with a note, written with the patient's agreement, saying that the psychotherapist or counsellor found the patient to be in a very distressed state and wished to refer the patient, believing that an emergency psychiatric referral would be most helpful. The practitioner may need to say no more than this, and so confidentiality is maintained. However there may need to be a fuller confidential discussion with the EAP, mentioning the practitioner's own diagnosis of the situation. This example illustrates how difficult it can be to maintain absolute confidentiality while also caring for the patient in the most appropriate way.

The approach of the major psychotherapy and counselling organizations, which has been favoured over the years, has been to work in a more pragmatic way that assumes that confidentiality is all-important, while ensuring that patients understand the limits of the confidentiality on offer and recognize that practitioners do not work in isolation. Some employers may require disclosure of particular types of information through their contracts of employment, and practitioners need to be aware of any such restriction on confidentiality prior to starting practice. There may also be instances where practitioners might be obliged by law to divulge confidential information.

Let us look first at the requirements of employers. Practitioners working for an employer may find themselves in a position of having to negotiate in a pragmatic way to establish a contract that is acceptable to both their employer and themselves. They will have duties to their patients, to themselves in terms of their professional codes of ethics, as well as responsibilities to their team and employer. The responsibilities inherent in such contracts need to be clearly laid out and understood by all parties.

An example of a situation that involves confidential issues could be that of the psychotherapist or counsellor working in a doctors' surgery. Kate is a counsellor working in a surgery where the doctor wants to have brief notes on the counselling sessions attached to the patient's file. Kate could take an absolutist position, refusing to discuss anything about the patient with the doctor, since she would consider that agreeing to such a request would lead to a breach of confidentiality. If Kate takes a more pragmatic position she will probably negotiate with the doctors at the start of her work at the surgery what they, Kate and any other concerned parties collectively feel are the limits of confidentiality, taking into consideration the code of ethics and practice she is working under. They will need to agree as well how confidential material will be stored and managed. Once this has been decided, any limits to confidentiality will need to be made known to patients who come for counselling.

Just as the doctors need to respect the degree of confidentiality that Kate feels her work requires, she must also respect the doctors' need to know. The doctors need enough information to satisfy them that their patients are not deteriorating, and, since counselling is their treatment of choice, that they are responding well enough and do not need additional treatment. Kate may need to ask whose patients they are. Are they the doctor's patients whom she is contracted by the doctor to work with? Or is she the practitioner and therefore a free agent? Or is she a team or practice member?

Kate has dual accountability to patient and employer. Therefore she must have a clear contract with the medical practice and then reflect this in making contracts with her patients. In the example given, it would seem wise for Kate to see herself as a team practice member and her contracts need to reflect this. In this case, the patients' notes are the property of the surgery. Kate needs to make sure that they are stored suitably, so that the ring of confidentiality is as restricted as possible. What is recorded in the notes is then a matter of Kate's discretion. She needs to be mindful that these notes reflect her clinical responsibility and accountability to her patients, and that they will have access to them under the Access to Health Records Act 1990. Therefore she needs to consider:

- what she intends to record and in what form;
- why she is recording it;
- whether the record is official or personal;
- who will have rights of access, including third parties such as insurance companies.

Kate may also wish to keep additional process notes, noting her personal responses to sessions, which would focus on her own development as a counsellor. They would note her personal reactions, transference, counter-transference and other observations and reflections for supervision purposes. They would be stored by Kate. This arrangement also needs to be agreed in advance with other members of the team.

All too often confusion, distress and disagreements arise because these matters have not been fully thought through at the beginning of employment. The practitioner's need for maintaining confidentiality and close handling of information may be perceived as being critical of the system that is already in place. These matters are inclined to become personalized or mixed up with other disagreements, and relationships within the team break down. It is important to be both knowledgeable of and understanding of the established culture of the host organization. The constraints on confidentiality which are seen as good practice among psychotherapists and counsellors are not automatically shared in other cultures, and, in a medical setting, may be perceived as bad practice, fostering a sense of distance and secrecy.

When moving to work in a culture that is not that of psychotherapy or counselling it is important that practitioners negotiate in a pragmatic way, keeping a keen eye on their own professional values. In this way the employer, whether it is a medical centre, school, college, or a youth service, can be helped to understand their point of view.

There are a number of legal considerations that prescribe the limits to confidentiality. The law respects the right to confidentiality in the medical and other professions. In *Hunter* v. *Mann* (1974) it was stated: 'Medical practitioners and others in a similar position . . . are bound by a duty which the law respects and enforces, from disclosing without the consent of the patient or client, communications or information obtained in a professional capacity, save in certain exceptional circumstances in the public interest.' The duty of confidentiality is stated in the following way in 'Counselling, Confidentiality and the Law',[1] 'Legally and ethically there is a strong expectation that counsellors will maintain confidentiality as a general principle'. The entitlement to confidentiality is enforceable in common law.

A patient can sue in the County Court for breach of confidentiality, whether it is an express or implied contractual term. This is a relatively cheap and easy action to bring which is usually available to clients who pay fees for their counselling. The courts may well uphold a duty of confidentiality, particularly if the nature of the relationship implies that it will be confidential, or if the communication was accepted in confidence, or if the patient asks that what is about to be told be kept secret.

There can however be defensible breaches of confidentiality, for example:

- when the patient gives consent;
- when the confidences disclosed are already public knowledge;
- on 'public interest' grounds, as there are statutory obligations in some cases relating to crime, suicide and young people.

In statute law itself there are now certain references to confidentiality in psychotherapy and counselling. For instance in the Police and Criminal Evidence Act 1984, counselling records are given extra protection, in that a search warrant to obtain access to records requires a circuit judge's signature rather than merely a magistrate's. The Human Fertilisation and Embryology Act 1990 requires counselling records to be kept confidential and separately from other records.

There are statutory obligations that are binding on the public and thus all practitioners. Principal among these are:

- the Prevention of Terrorism (Temporary Provisions) Act which has been renewed annually;
- the Children Act 1989, which puts practitioners 'under a qualified duty to assist in child welfare inquiries';
- the Mental Health Act 1983, when the patient may be a danger to himself or another person.

These are all complex areas and the practitioner should think carefully, and consult his or her supervisor in the first instance before taking any action that would breach confidentiality. In many cases advice may need to be taken from the practitioner's insurer, or a solicitor suggested by the

---

[1]   Bond, T. and the Standards and Ethics Sub-Committee (1994) BAC Info Guide 1.

insurer, or from the professional organization. Anonymous advice can also be taken from social workers, or specific organizations such as the NSPCC, or the Children's Legal Advice Centre.

Any breach of confidentiality, whether defensible or obligatory, will cause considerable difficulty and concern for a practitioner. A practitioner who feels that it may be necessary to breach confidentiality should, if at all feasible, speak to the patient about these concerns. This is possible in most cases; for example, if a patient is suicidal or the practitioner is concerned about the duty of care for children. However, it may not be possible and practitioners need to consider what they would do in these circumstances.

The following scenario gives a sense of the potential complexities in such a situation. In the early days of the Children Act, Jane was working as a part-time social worker and she was seeing a patient, John, in a counselling agency. He was speaking in particular about his recently broken marriage. John had now moved in with Mary, with whom he had been having a long-standing affair; she had two children, a daughter of eight and a son of five. John felt extremely guilty about the fact that his sexual attraction towards Mary had broken up his marriage. During the once-weekly sessions, John spoke more and more frequently of his sexual fantasies about Mary and increasingly about Mary's daughter. Jane and her supervisor were both concerned about the situation but felt it to be contained.

John came to the next session in a particularly depressed mood and talked more about Mary's daughter. At this point, Jane decided that she must breach confidentiality to ensure the safety of the daughter, who she feared had become the object of John's sexual advances. She contacted the relevant people, John was taken to the police station for questioning and the children were examined. Mary was distraught. The children were found to be unharmed and the police did not pursue the matter. This incident led not only to a complete breakdown of trust between John and his therapist, but also a breakdown of the delicate relationships in this new family of John, Mary and Mary's children. Mary, for her part, could not understand what John might have said that could have caused his therapist to approach the social services. She could no longer have confidence in him and their relationship broke down.

The case study raises several issues. First, every agency needs to have a policy as to whether or not it is governed specifically by the Children Act. If it is funded by a Local Authority or a Health Authority there may be no choice in this matter, as that particular legal obligation may come with the funding. Any decision on action in such a case is then not a

LIBRARY, UNIVERSITY COLLEGE CHESTER

matter for individual discretion but is governed by the policy of the agency.

If Jane had seen John in a private practice she could have decided on a policy in response to the perceived crisis. An independent practitioner is under no statutory obligation, and can therefore respond to the particular situation from her own moral position, having considered and been informed by conventions of good practice.

Second, we come to a practice issue; that the practitioner was not able to contain her own anxiety and hold to her therapeutic role. It was the breaching of confidentiality and the failure to keep a therapeutic stance which lead to a disastrous set of consequences. Let us consider what went wrong. The case highlights the delicate balance that practitioners have to maintain between their clients' outer and inner worlds. A young girl or woman may be very attractive to her step-father but there is a considerable difference between fantasy and acting out, and it is up to the practitioner to hold and contain this. It is also the work of a supervisor to contain and monitor such a situation, by bringing in a third eye, the balancing eye, that can help the practitioner to ask the appropriate questions. The supervisor or consultant is essential as well in considering the implications of differing courses of action, or finding a new perspective. If the suspicions had been discussed with the patient he might have responded in a way that convinced the practitioner that he had not acted out his fantasy. It would also have helped the patient to ground himself in reality, and react to the misunderstanding between the practitioner and himself.

We have seen that confidentiality is a vital ingredient in psychotherapeutic work; and yet patients' confidences may, in their best interests and with their knowledge, be shared with supervisors or with practitioners' employers.

To breach confidentiality is a crucial matter. Any practitioner who does it needs to be sure that it is justifiable and that he or she can convince a tribunal or court that the action was defensible or obligatory. The duty of confidentiality forms part of a legally enforceable contract and affects such aspects of contract-making as client consent, supervision, training, research and intellectual property. If the practitioner is concerned about possibly breaching confidentiality, it may be advisable to consult a third party, such as a supervisor or possibly an insurer, in order to decide on the best course of action.

# Chapter 5

# Mistakes or malpractice

In this chapter we will try to distinguish between mistakes, poor practice, negligence and malpractice. There is a considerable difference between these four concepts, essentially in degrees of intent.

## MISTAKES

A *mistake* is an unintended slip in good practice. An example of a mistake might be: a counselling agency leaves its answerphone on during August, and one of those who is responsible for monitoring the phone forgets to check it so that a potential patient is left with a call unanswered for ten days. The potential patient then faces a long wait for an assessment session, which is usual in the agency, but feels aggrieved by a sense of not being attended to.

Mistakes in training organizations and in agencies providing psychotherapy and counselling often arise because of breakdowns in the administrative system. Nearly all organizations and agencies are run by a number of part-time workers, sometimes one full-time worker, and often there is insufficient administrative support because of lack of adequate funding. Often, if an agency wishes to appear to its potential patients to be less formal than a clinic in the Health Service, the administrative system is either purposely hidden from the potential patient or, more commonly, located largely in the heads of one or two individuals. Such systems need only a little disturbance, say someone being ill for a few days, for the agency to falter and leave the potential patient feeling uncontained.

Let us consider the practitioner who needs to take a day off in the week after next to go to a colleague's funeral. The practitioner forgets to tell the patient until the first session in the following week. The patient is cross, having during the weekend turned down an offer of a day at the races because of the scheduled therapy session. This occurrence needs attention from the practitioner's point of view, but it is not a mistake. However, if the session has been cancelled by the patient to attend a funeral, another offered by the practitioner in lieu, and then the practitioner forgets the session, it would be a mistake.

## POOR PRACTICE

*Poor practice* is a failure of good practice, whether intentional or not. This most often happens in areas of contract-making and confidentiality where, while there is no desire to mislead or to breach confidentiality, there is, nevertheless, carelessness or a real breakdown of good practice. In essence it is a failure to pay due care and attention to practice standards that the practitioner knows are required.

Some of the most complex examples of poor practice happen when a practitioner is suddenly taken ill, is involved in an accident or dies. Unless records are kept in order and colleagues know where these records are, difficulties arise. For instance, a practitioner, George, living in Reading, was working with a patient, Rory, who was a counsellor. Rory was teaching a developmental psychology course in Newbury and at the end of the course one of his students, Sue, came up to him saying that her father was a psychotherapist, mentioning George's name. There is already a confusion of boundaries here but one that cannot be helped since the only person who could possibly have known about the student's familial relationship was George, who was bound by confidentiality. However when subsequently George had a heart attack, no one in his family knew what to do about his patients. They decided to go through his diary and telephone them. Thus it happened that Sue telephoned Rory, saying 'Are you Rory? Do you see my father George? He has had a heart attack. I will telephone you in a week to say how he is and when he can see you next. I think I recognize your voice, are you the Rory who teaches me in Newbury?' Because George had not made a proper arrangement for a colleague to manage his practice in the event of his ill-health or accident, the identity of his patient was compromised.

Poor practice can happen when confidentiality is not maintained in an agency. For example, a practitioner answers the telephone to a patient, and hearing the patient's name as Duncan Smith says 'Oh, yes, you are my colleague Mary Rose's patient aren't you?' The practitioner, even though she may have been privy to this knowledge through the agency's record system, should have waited for the patient to confirm his or her therapist's name. The poor practice may not seem intentional on the practitioner's part: she may wish to be seen by the patient to be providing a secure environment. However she did reveal that she knew of the therapeutic relationship between Duncan Smith and Mary Rose.

It is poor practice to keep clinical records in the same place as the patient's name, address and telephone number. A file might be left on a tube, train or bus and another person may pick it up and read the contents. They may even know to whom it refers. It is far better practice to keep clinical notes that may be needed for supervision, or must be carried from place to place, separate from the names, addresses and telephone numbers of the patients concerned.

It is also poor practice for a patient repeatedly to turn up for sessions and find that the practitioner, a consultant psychotherapist, has been held up at her hospital clinic. She should allow adequate time to travel home and to be there to receive the patient.

## Poor practice in training institutions

It is now usual for providers of training and trainees to have a contract between them. The contract sets out what the course providers should deliver in terms of teaching and, in turn, the students know what work is expected of them and the standard that will be necessary for qualification.

As courses comply with national standards being set by accrediting bodies, who in their turn are conforming to the requirements of the umbrella organizations, professional practice education improves and fewer of these kinds of problems arise. However, where they exist, they often result from a trainer not being a practitioner and therefore not being able to model the orientation of therapy that is being taught. Likewise there are training supervisors who may not be clinical practitioners themselves but come from some other specialism. They may get caught up in the dynamics between the practitioner and patient and fail to realize that the practitioner's difficulties may be being reflected in the dynamics between themselves and the practitioner. This is often referred to as the parallel process.

In the past there have been courses where, without previous warning, or without the possibility even being raised in the course literature, staff have told students to repeat a year or suggested an extra year of training or more personal therapy. Trainees may feel that those running the course will gain personally from prolonging their training, and this may be true, particularly if the course is run by a private company. The question is, does the additional training or therapy answer the training needs of the student? There is an obligation on trainers and assessors to be very sure of their own judgement in situations where they might financially benefit from extending or delaying the completion of a student's training.

## Poor practice by trainers

Trainers need to consider what their contract is with the students and with the institution. A large element of therapeutic training is the way in which the trainer models the work. It is now far less acceptable in the teaching world generally for lecturers and tutors to view their students as potential companions, partners or lovers. This is particularly true in the psychotherapy and counselling professions. The training relationship has plenty of potential for emotional bad practice. Take the case where the tutor takes the trainee home in his or her car, or walks with him or her to the bus stop, or meets up with one particular trainee in the pub to have a drink. The student may feel that he or she is very special because of this preferential treatment. In turn, these circumstances can feed the transference and unexpected and painful emotions may arise which the trainer then feels unable to handle. Sometimes he or she does try to handle the situation and gets deeper and deeper into difficulties with the trainee.

The tutor also risks even greater confusion in the mind of the trainee if he or she allows or gives a kiss at the end of the journey. The nature of the kiss and whether or how it is returned can be a further complication.

Other examples of bad practice can arise when trainers fail to notice when a trainee is near breakdown or when his or her personal circumstances are impinging to an unacceptable level on their training or on clinical work that is part of the training. Trainees need to be advised by their trainers if they perceive that the trainees' work with patients is not satisfactory, or that there is a danger that they may not successfully complete the training. The trainees have made a considerable commitment of time and money to the training and expect to complete it in the usual time unless otherwise advised.

## Poor practice in supervision

Supervisors are very powerful in training. Depending on the school or orientation, the supervisor will hold more or less power. Some supervisors work with tape recordings of clinical sessions and may even record the sessions with their supervisees. Supervisors from psychodynamic orientations hold power particularly because there is no other check, such as tape recording, of either the session with the patient or of the supervision session, which would allow another view of what might be going on in either the consulting room or the supervisor's room. It is also unusual in such traditions for a training committee to take a different view from the supervisor, or to change supervision for the trainee. It is therefore vitally important that supervisors are particularly careful about parallel processes between themselves and their supervisees, and take consultative support if they are having difficulties with any particular trainee.

It is very rare to have a complaint by a patient against a supervisor though there may be grounds in law since the supervisor could be considered to have sufficient knowledge of the therapy for them to be included in any case of negligence against a practitioner or trainee. Supervisors are responsible for the work they supervise and it is often felt by investigators, mediators and adjudicators of complaints against practitioners, that they would have liked to have had the opportunity to discuss with the practitioner's supervisor why the difficulties in the work were not picked up in supervision or managed better between the practitioner and supervisor.

## NEGLIGENCE

*Negligence* is a want of proper care or attention and involves carelessness. Aspects of negligence can be seen in many of the examples that were used in the last section. Further examples might be: the practitioner who fails to lodge or return a report to a GP about a suicidal patient when the doctor has requested that he is informed if the patient becomes more desperate; or the supervisor who goes away for an extended period of teaching or supervising and does not provide his or her supervisees with adequate alternative care; or the trainer who knows that a trainee is in a personal crisis and does not intervene and stop the trainee practising. Each of these scenarios involves lack of care or attention to the responsibilities of the role the practitioner is in, in relation to the patient, supervisee or trainee.

## MALPRACTICE

*Malpractice* is generally defined as practice or behaviour that is intentionally, emotionally, financially, physically or sexually abusive. It also includes behaviour within a training organization or placement agency that is financially or sexually exploitative. In medical and other settings it would be referred to as professional or gross professional misconduct. It is the act of engaging in practice with malicious intent with the specific aim of neglecting the practitioner's professional duty through intentionally unethical professional conduct. It is generally taken to mean behaviour which is knowingly wrong. It usually involves a practitioner following a course of action designed to meet his or her own needs.

The practitioner may claim he or she is acting in the patient's best interests or on a basis of mutual consent. Such claims are almost invariably made, the practitioner being unable to contemplate that he or she may have acted wrongly. Whatever the attempted justification, it is an intentional, specific and calculated breach of proper professional conduct.

**Emotional malpractice**

Practitioners of whatever persuasion are usually aware of the power that they have in the therapeutic setting. In most traditions the practitioner reveals very little or nothing about him or herself, leaving the patient's conscious and unconscious worlds wide open to fantasize as they will. In the psychoanalytic and psychodynamic orientations in particular this is called transference.

These fantasies are a very powerful tool in the work done with patients but they also represent a power imbalance that needs to be treated with the greatest caution. It is often only by relating to the practitioner's own experience of transference, whether to a significant individual in his or her life or his or her own experience of therapy, that the practitioner knows its real power. It has become the established practice for some practitioners to use the considerable power of the relationship to draw patients into further involvement with themselves by, for example, involving them in training schemes or workshops that they are running; or they may involve them in ways which can be improper, say by developing social relationships with them or receiving services from them, such as servicing a car, or greater financial involvements such as selling the patient a car, or involving loans of money or property or even the sale of a house.

In any financial matter where close personal relationships are involved it is hard for those involved to be objective. Let us consider the example of a practitioner who offers a session in return for house cleaning. The therapy session may be valued at £24 per hour while the cleaning might be valued at £4 per hour. In other words the patient has to work for six hours in order to pay the practitioner for one hour's work. This is a revealing imbalance of power, whether it is viewed symbolically or actually, leaving aside the fact that cleaning up after another person involves an imbalance of power in itself. More importantly, from the psychotherapeutic point of view, is the breach of boundaries which brings the patient into the practitioner's private world where he or she should not be and probably has no desire to be.

Baby-sitting and child care are other services which have been offered in exchange for therapy. This is particularly inappropriate and may upset the patients in particular because it is often his or her 'baby' parts that the patient needs and wishes to attend to in therapy. Practitioners who involve themselves in arrangements of this kind need to consider what they are doing in terms of their developing therapeutic relationship with the patient. It would be far more appropriate for the patient to do housework or baby-sit for someone else and then negotiate an appropriate fee with the practitioner.

Another kind of abuse of power can take place when a practitioner offers a patient things that he or she needs, such as clothes or furniture. The patient may feel the power imbalance – 'I have less than she does' – as well as an obligation to be grateful to the practitioner, confusing the relationship, particularly the transference.

The therapy becomes contaminated and compromised by such practices. The emotions aroused are quite different from any fantasy that the patient may have in relation to the practitioner and the very concreteness of the action makes it extremely difficult to work with. Some of the examples overlap with the next category.

**Financial malpractice**

This area of malpractice is a concerning one, not only because the giving of money in exchange for the practitioner's services is an important matter to work with in therapy, but also because it helps to maintain the proper boundaries between the practitioner as the provider of a service and the patient as the purchaser of that service. Where the financial boundaries are not strictly observed the patient is being manipulated.

Take, for example, a case where a financial contract has been made with a patient with a date set for review but the practitioner decides nevertheless to ask for an increase in fees at an earlier stage. Or take a case where fees have been increased repeatedly. One patient was initially seen in a clinic setting, but when the practitioner left the clinic it was decided that the patient would move with the practitioner. At the clinic the original fee was set according to a formula based on the patient's earnings. After the patient had settled in at the new premises and while some very distressing material for the patient was emerging, the fee was raised. It was then raised twice more, to a level which, although it was proper for the practitioner to be charging, was twice as much as the fee charged in the clinic. The practitioner needs to consider whether this kind of fee-raising is a justifiable change of contract, and whether the patient is being treated fairly considering his or her emotionally vulnerable position. If the original fee was a term of the contract such a raising of the fee would in any case legally be considered as a breach of contract unless the client agreed to it or the review was provided for in the original contract.

Some patients wish to pay in cash for their sessions. However, they may well fantasize that the practitioner is not declaring the income to the Inland Revenue. It is therefore wise, as with all transactions, for the practitioner to give a fee note or receipt to the patient and to keep a record of all payments. Then the fees are dealt with in a financial way and the fantasies can be dealt with in a therapeutic way.

Suppose a patient decided to buy a house, not knowing that the person selling it was the nephew of his or her practitioner. It would be malpractice if the practitioner encouraged the patient to buy the house at a price advantageous to her nephew. Or, if a practitioner were to leave his sports car outside his practice with a note on it saying that it was for sale at a particular price, he would be unwise to sell it to a patient since it would be hard for them to bargain over the price in a detached way. The practitioner would expose himself to possible charges of financial malpractice.

### Physical malpractice

Some therapies, such as Gestalt, use touch as part of the work, while other traditions strictly avoid it. Therefore, if it is to be part of the therapy, the significance of touch needs to be understood by the patient. Even in the therapies that do use touch there can be, and have been, misunderstandings. The body therapist who gets down on the floor and touches or massages the abdomen or intimate parts of the patient needs to understand why he or she is doing so and the possible consequences. Can the patient tolerate the intimacy? Such therapists are normally alone in the room with their patient and, particularly in the early stages of the work, intimate touch, like the touching of a breast, may be misunderstood.

Of course touch can take place outside the therapies of which it is part. In this case it needs to be carefully considered. The touching of an arm when the patient is very distressed or newly bereaved is sometimes part of being sympathetic. When touch goes further than this practitioners really need to reflect on why it is happening and whether they believe it to be appropriate.

Sexual contact can be experienced in the practitioner's kiss and touch by the patient. Consider the case of a woman who had never had any sexual contact working with a practitioner who felt that she was too controlled. He perceived her as frigid and decided that sexual arousal would be 'good for her'. Thus over the weeks he made increasing moves towards having physical contact with her, by touching her and kissing and then touching her breasts. Gradually she became more confused and upset and challenged him. His reaction was to become very frightened and break off the therapy. The woman's confusion caused her to be very distressed and her friends suggested she see another practitioner. In working on what happened in the first therapy the patient felt able to make a complaint about the totally inappropriate behaviour of the first practitioner. The question that this raises for those of us who investigate or adjudicate such cases is whether such behaviour is ever valid.

What does need acknowledging here is that it is the patient's perception that matters; and if there can possibly be confusion the practitioner needs to clarify what he or she is doing and not persist with an approach that could be confusing for the patient. If physical contact is to be part of the therapy it needs to be discussed as part of the initial contract and its limits defined.

Malpractice when involving overt sexual activity is particularly powerful in therapy, as has been shown by Peter Rutter[1] and Gary Schoener.[2] The therapeutic alliance between practitioner and client evokes, consciously and unconsciously, early relationships, particularly those with the mother and father, in the transference. When sexual abuse of any kind takes place it touches the very earliest experiences in the client and the therapist's seeming concern fills the void left in the client by their inadequate childhood relationships. Sadly, the client who has had to endure sexual malpractice by their therapist has often already been the subject of sexual or physical abuses in childhood and thus becomes easy prey for practitioners who abuse clients in this way.

---

[1]  Rutter, P. (1989) *Sex in the Forbidden Zone*, London: Aquarian.
[2]  Schoener, G. (1994) 'Assessment and Rehabilitation of Professionals who have Engaged in Sexual Misconduct', paper given to British Psychological Society.

These findings are reinforced by the experience of the Prevention of Professional Abuse Network (POPAN), who are in touch with a considerable number of patients in Britain who have experienced abuse by their therapists. These patients are, like those in the Rutter and Schoener research, unwilling to bring complaints because they still need to believe themselves to be 'the very special' one in the eyes of their therapist. They may even need to hang on to this fantasy when they know that there have been other people in the same situation as themselves, having therapy and sex with the same practitioner. They also have the same kind of fear as people who have been raped; of shame, of not being believed, and of exposing themselves to scrutiny and blame.

**Sexual malpractice**

Sexual malpractice can take many forms, from intimate touch to full sexual intercourse. All the umbrella organizations' guidelines for codes of ethics say that any sexual contact with a patient is inappropriate. It is important for practitioners to remember that if sexual feelings are aroused it is very often a key time in working with a patient. If the feelings that are aroused cannot be worked with for what they are, then the therapy needs to become a matter for supervision, because these feelings need to be understood in terms of the projections and counter-projections involved in the therapeutic work and not acted out in some inappropriate manner. Should the feelings themselves become uncontainable then the practitioner needs to cease working with the patient.

There are some variations in the views of different schools of therapy as to whether a sexual relationship may be entered into at a later time. A number would say that there needs to be a period of discretion, while other groups, namely the psychoanalytically orientated and psycho-dynamic groups, would see the work very much with the transference in mind and would feel that a sexual relationship with a past patient was unacceptable at any stage because the transference could still be active. They would say that the practitioner in this situation needed to review his or her position and discover some understanding of the predicament through therapy or analysis since the imbalance of power in the relationship remains even when the therapy has ended.

## Institutional incest

There are therapeutic organizations, as there are religious and other sects, where having sexual intercourse with the guru or leader is part of the initiation. In therapeutic organizations, when sexual relations between senior practitioners and their trainees become endemic, the practice does not normally cease when the first group of students qualify but can continue to the third and fourth generation. This is known as institutional incest.

Such groups are not members of the national umbrella organizations, for if they were, they would immediately be the subject of investigation. They act like secret sects and have all the problems and the abusive power issues of such sects. They do, however, bring the profession into considerable disrepute because they use the terms 'psychotherapy' and 'counselling' in describing themselves.

Many of us may, on reflection, be able to think of examples of mistakes and possibly of poor practice in our personal experience, for instance the morning when we overslept, or the phone call we wish we had returned. Often a failure of good practice may occur with the best of intentions, or simply through carelessness or a failure to observe appropriate boundaries. Practitioners must be ever vigilant in their professional relationships, whether with patients, trainees, supervisees or employers, to maintain a professional stance. What is certain is that any clear cases of negligence and malpractice do damage to us all, and bring the entire profession into disrepute.

# Chapter 6

# Grievances, complaints and protecting the fair name of the profession

A complaints procedure exists primarily for the protection of the public, but also to protect the fair name of the profession. Any professional group needs to consider who can legitimately bring a complaint, and this is particularly important in counselling and psychotherapy. In these days of free access to complaints systems the expected answer might be that anyone has the right to complain. However, as a professional group, we need to consider what is fair and just and best serves our 'stakeholders', the patients, and those working with them.

It is usual that a complaint is brought by those who receive services, in other words patients, trainees and supervisees. Therapeutic umbrella organizations generally do not accept complaints from third parties, that is, individuals who are outside the contractual relationship and who are not receiving the services. This is because there have been, in the past, cases where the information gained by a third party during a hearing was released to the press or otherwise became public knowledge, to the detriment of the other parties concerned. It was felt that such public exposure did no one any good, particularly the patient. It was also felt that practitioners needed protection against third party complaints. They are particularly vulnerable in divorce proceedings, when an irate partner may turn against the patient's therapist, seeing him or her as holding vital information about the partner or being the reason for the breakdown of the marriage.

As a result of such an experience one umbrella organization decided that in future only the purchaser of the services, the patient, trainee or supervisee should be able to pursue a complaint. If a matter of misconduct is heard about, via a third party, there remains the opportunity of pursuing the matter through the Articles of Association of an organization. The Articles of most professional organizations include a clause which allows the organization to remove from membership any individual or organization that brings the profession into disrepute. If any third party, whether it is a member of the public or the media, provides clear and substantial evidence to the professional body of wrongdoing by a member, the practitioner can be temporarily de-registered, or have his or her membership withdrawn, pending an appeal. Thus most organizations have a clear fall-back position to enable them to deal with a third party. In most organizations within the British Association for Counselling (BAC), the British Confederation of Psycho-therapists (BCP) and the United Kingdom Council for Psychotherapy (UKCP) these arrangements hold true.

Let us look at some examples. A member of a professional organ-ization is exposed in the press as having a history of abusive behaviour; or a court case exposes a member's financial wrongdoing; or two or three trainees 'whistle blow' about sexual misconduct within a counselling agency. In the first case there might be corroborative evidence such as social services or police records, knowledge of which would be needed if a professional organization were to invoke its Articles of Association and remove the practitioner from membership. In the second case, there would need to be a considerable amount of clear evidence to satisfy the legal burden of proof and then the organization might well wish to deal with it in the same way. In the third case, where there is alleged serious sexual misconduct within an agency, the umbrella organization concerned would need to consider whether there is adequate evidence against the agency for it to act. It might prefer to pursue a complaint against the agency itself, or support those who came to it reporting what was happening, if they were in some way involved, rather than invoking the Articles of Association. However, it might feel that there is ample evidence and proceed to remove the practitioner or organization from membership. The principle that needs to be considered here, as in all cases of misconduct, is that the more serious the offence the more thoroughly and unambiguously it needs to be proved. If there is not sufficient proof it might be better to pursue a 'one-step' complaints procedure rather than possibly involve the organization in a counter-claim of libel or for loss of earnings.

If a practitioner is removed from membership in this way, there needs to be a system by which he or she can appeal against the decision of the management committee, council or governing board of the organization. An appeal board needs to be seen as independent, respectful of the principles of natural justice, and capable of making its own decisions on the evidence presented to it. The onus of proof rests with the appellant to clear his or her name, since those who made the original decision to remove the practitioner from membership were convinced of the necessity to do so to protect the fair name of the profession. The appeals panel will be expected to have a clear view at the end of their deliberations and make decisions about the sanction, whether to uphold or disallow the exclusion, and, if they uphold it, about the length of time the practitioner should be excluded from membership before re-application might be considered.

Apart from the Articles of the Association there are two different kinds of process which may be used if someone who receives a service wishes to express a sense of injury or injustice. These are usually dealt with through either grievance procedures or complaints procedures.

A *grievance procedure* is generally the best method of dealing with a problem which arises *within* an institution. In the psychotherapy profession this usually means a training organization or an agency offering placements and providing therapy services to the public. Grievances can normally be dealt with in-house, fairly speedily, and often a resolution can be reached. Grievances normally concern internal difficulties; trainee with trainer, trainee with supervisor, volunteer with agency or agency with volunteer. Should resolution not be possible then the matter might become a complaint; but it is important from a legal point of view that the proper channels have been exhausted before the aggrieved person moves on to using a complaints procedure.

There are occasions when the grievance processes within an organization do not function or the aggrieved person believes the process is unsafe for them to use. Such a situation might occur when there is a climate of fear within an organization, or a culture of corruption or 'laissez-faire' which allows poor or bad practice to flourish. At some level within the organization there is a collusion which allows the situation to persist and individuals are loath to reveal unethical practices or question the way things are done. In such an organization grievance procedures would be unsafe to use.

A grievance procedure is intended to provide a quick independent look at a situation that no longer feels fair or safe to the aggrieved party. These procedures are now used widely in the work place. The organization needs to be sure when setting up a grievance procedure that the person with the grievance is not penalized, that the organization will act presuming his or her genuineness, that it can be seen to have created positive channels for the expression of concerns and that it is ready to explain its decisions and work in a consensus-building way. If the aggrieved person feels no confidence in the organization to manage the grievance in a fair and impartial way then he or she has the option of using the complaints procedure. There is, therefore, good reason for organizations to have proper grievance procedures because they are simpler and consequently quicker, causing less disruption and stress within the agency itself. Many psychotherapy and counselling organizations already have them in place.

The procedure usually consists of two parts. First, an informal meeting is held between senior members of the organization who are not directly involved in the grievance. They listen to the grievance and respond by reflecting what is said and offering their understanding of the situation. If mediation and conciliation are then thought to be possible, the person bringing the grievance and the person against whom it is brought will meet those hearing the grievance to try to reach a compromise or solution. These processes can all take place at one extended meeting, though two separate meetings may be necessary.

If the matter cannot be resolved in such a way then a formal meeting will need to be arranged. A panel of, say, three people will be convened, possibly including the director of the organization, a member of staff at the same level as the person expressing the grievance or the person against whom the grievance is expressed, and a member of the board of management. Should the grievance be about a particularly serious matter or involve a number of members of the organization, then it would be seen as good practice for an independent person to be involved who is not a member of the professional organization.

Let us look at some examples. A counsellor who is working as a volunteer within a counselling agency has asked to work with three patients, which is the usual number for the agency. After four months the other counsellors who volunteered at the same time as she did have three patients but she has only one. One of her original three attended once only and the third never came. The volunteer brings this to supervision; her supervisor is employed by the training organization and shares the volunteer's concern that she is not getting the experience she needs. It is in the back of both of their minds that 150 hours of experience is needed for the volunteer to complete her course requirements within the next eighteen months and at present she has only ten hours' experience. The supervisor encourages the volunteer to speak to the counselling co-ordinator about her predicament, which she does. However nothing changes, even after two further attempts.

At this point the volunteer feels that her relationship with the counselling co-ordinator has broken down and she decides that she needs to register a grievance with the management group of the agency. She wonders if she is not being allocated patients because the counselling co-ordinator has a concern about her competence. She knows that, if necessary, she still has time to look for another placement in order to complete her course requirements.

The manager of the agency meets the volunteer to discuss her grievance and discovers that she feels she is under pressure from her course and from her supervisor, who is one of the course team staff and not a member of the agency staff, to complete her placement and qualify. Later the manager finds out that the course's funding depends partly on numbers on the course and partly on students completing courses satisfactorily. The manager speaks to the counselling co-ordinator, who feels that the volunteer has become unnerved by the second patient leaving after the first session and the third patient's non-attendance. He wanted the volunteer to consolidate her work with her first patient so that he could feel confident about passing another patient to her. The co-ordinator points out forcibly that patients are not fodder for volunteers who are doing training courses, that his first responsibility is to the patients and that unless and until he has confidence in the volunteer's work, he will not pass further patients to her.

After some discussion the manager discovers that this outburst on the co-ordinator's part comes from the growing pressure he, too, feels himself to be under from the course. The manager can then negotiate and bring volunteer and co-ordinator together. She emphasizes to the volunteer the need to put the interests of the patients first and protect the integrity of the service and explains that more than eighteen months may be needed to complete her placement. To the co-ordinator she suggests that if he now has sufficient confidence in the volunteer he might allocate another patient to her. The manager also acknowledges to both parties the pressure from the training organization, but suggests that this needs to be considered as a separate issue by the management committee, who may need to review the policy of the agency or negotiate with the organization to see if changes are needed.

If the manager was unable to resolve this matter in an informal way and the co-ordinator had decided to stick to his opinion that the volunteer should have no more patients for the present, the volunteer would have to decide whether to leave the matter there and be delayed in qualifying, or to request that her grievance be formally heard. In this case the manager would need to inform the management group and its chair-person would then convene a formal hearing. The chairperson might chair the panel, and ask another volunteer and the director of a similar placement agency to be members. The hearing could follow the format of a complaints investigation and would hear the grievance of the volunteer and the response of the co-ordinator. The panel would then decide whether the volunteer's or the co-ordinator's point of view should be upheld and what should be the result.

*Complaints procedures* are used to protect the public and the fair name of the profession, by maintaining the very high standards expected from those who are either registered with, or members of, our professional bodies. Complainants usually belong to one of three discrete groups, the first being the patients, members of the public who are receiving services from professional members. The second group consists of those who are in psychotherapy, counselling or supervision as part of a training. A complaint by a trainee or supervisee against a training therapist or trainer could possibly be dealt with through a grievance procedure, but the trainee may feel that the only way to be heard in an independent way is to complain and thus involve the observing eye of an individual or professional body outside their own organization. Trainees may feel particularly vulnerable, fearing that, if they challenge their therapy, complaints may be seen as unresolved transference issues or conscious or unconscious problems with authority and they may risk failing their training. The third group of people who may make a complaint against practitioners are their colleagues. Complaints by one practitioner about the practice of another are common and, increasingly, are acted upon. This kind of difficulty can be very painful because the practitioners often know each other as colleagues or friends. It is often only after considerable heart-searching that such complaints are expressed. This kind of complaint is most often brought against an older practitioner whose ways have not kept up with the current thinking about what constitutes professional behaviour. The experience of receiving a complaint from a fellow professional can have a very severe impact on a practitioner.

The act of alleging malpractice by a colleague can never be free from powerful and often quite primitive emotions. As camps form supporting the complainant or complained against, oppositional dynamics may completely take over and a state of 'impasse' result. An awareness of the impact of complaining can in itself act as a severe deterrent. However, it may be very important for one or two colleagues to make a complaint in order to protect the reputation of their professional organization.

When practitioners are aware of circumstances which, they believe, jeopardize patients either in an individual's practice or within an organization they may need to 'whistle blow'. This is a matter of their personal accountability as professionals; if they do not act they will be equally guilty of misconduct by not taking action. Whistle blowers believe something to be morally amiss and that it is necessary to protect the patient's interests. They believe the normal channels of communication are no longer possible and, therefore, see an independent investigation as the only way to protect the fair name of their profession.

There can be conflict between a practitioner's role as a professional and as an employee, for instance in a college or in the health service, where resources are limited. Therefore it is particularly important for the practitioner who feels that he or she needs to whistle blow to be sure that they know what their boundaries and roles are before doing so. Whistle blowers are unusual in therapeutic organizations and agencies, but in the future there may need to be more if high standards and ethical practice are to be maintained. If, on the other hand, there are grievance and complaints procedures that work smoothly and well in most organizations there are likely to be few whistle blowers, since they will feel that they can follow just and clear procedures and get a fair outcome.

An example of this can be seen where a complaint was made against a senior practitioner, Samuel, who, two of his supervisees said, was talking in their supervision sessions about matters that he could only know about through working in therapy with a third member of the course. The supervisees were well acquainted with the ethical conventions that are usual in the work and decided to discuss the matter with a younger and highly reputable trainer, George. George knew and respected Samuel as a practitioner who did good therapeutic work with difficult client groups. However, over the past three years he had been approached several times by other practitioners and trainees about breaches of confidence by Samuel. The two supervisees could give George clear evidence and George took it upon himself to make a formal complaint to Samuel's professional organization because he felt that Samuel's behaviour was damaging the name of counselling in the local community.

Should all channels of complaint feel closed to the potential complainant then the complainant might directly approach the umbrella organization, claiming that what is being told is a justifiable disclosure. A disclosure is said to be justifiable when it can arguably be seen to do more good than harm and serve some purpose in correcting or preventing the wrongdoing concerned, when it is made in a responsible manner and where it follows upon the exhaustion of internal channels or complaint and redress. This might result, in the case of a complaint, in taking the matter outside the organization where it arose, or it might even lead to revealing wrongdoing to the press because the complainant has not found other channels through which to express his or her concerns. It is therefore imperative that grievance and complaints procedures are known about and available to those who might wish to use them.

All grievances and complaints, whoever invokes them, need to be able to be handled with clear and credible processes and procedures that address these issues of private or public concern. It is essential to be seen by everyone, public and professionals alike, to be dealing with such matters in a positive and open way. This is a vital element in maintaining public confidence in the profession.

# Chapter 7

# A complaint from a patient

When, one morning, a letter drops on to the doormat and the practitioner, Jaz, opens it to find that Joy, a patient who recently suddenly stopped coming to see him, is complaining about her last sessions and asking for a refund of her fees, what should he do? This could be the beginning of a direct complaint from the patient.

Jaz should consider the situation very carefully. A cautious and well thought-out response is far better than an immediate reaction. It is better for the patient to wait a week for a considered reply rather than receiving a hasty one which might possibly provoke a strong counter-response which could ultimately lead to litigation. Careful handling of the complaint can prevent this.

It is often wise to confer with a colleague. An obvious choice might be Jaz's supervisor or consultant. The work with this patient may have been particularly attended to in their work together. However, it may also have been neglected and that would equally be reason for careful consideration. The practitioner needs to have his resources grouped around him and the confidential relationship of supervision is the single most appropriate support. The supervisor's advice may give the practitioner another view of what the patient is saying. It could be that Jaz and his supervisor have a particular view of this patient, and doubtless they will see the communication from Joy as part of her own process.

Another colleague whom Jaz might wish to consult is the person within his professional organization who is responsible for ethical issues, such as the chair of the ethics or complaints committee. He or she could be consulted for two reasons, first to get advice about how to handle the situation, and second to give the practitioner another view of what the patient is saying. The chair of the complaints committee, however, will be completely outside the therapeutic process and will not need to know anything of the clinical work that has been going on. His or her role is to advise on good practice and procedure or managing a problem, in this case one which could become a complaint.

The patient may decide to take the matter to Jaz's professional organization, or Jaz may wish to ask the patient to do so because he may feel that the professional organization needs to mediate in order to resolve the issue. Should the complainant be likely to be particularly vociferous it might serve the practitioner best to respond by suggesting that the matter could be dealt with by the complaints process of his professional body.

Another person Jaz should consider consulting is his insurer. It is essential that all practitioners should have professional insurance. Without it they are acting recklessly and may well be in breach of the ethical guidelines of their professional group. However, all too frequently, practitioners who are not insured have complaints made against them. Though there have not been many high-profile court cases in counselling and psychotherapy, there have been cases that have come up at Industrial and Race Relations Tribunals which have considered the behaviour and practice of practitioners. It is important that notification of a potential claim to insurers is prompt, since delay can be a ground for insurers denying liability and such cases are expensive. Above all an insurer can be a mine of information at a time like this, and many insurers will help with legal advice so that the practitioner can respond to a letter like Joy's with more confidence. It is worth checking in advance whether the insurer offers this service. Some do, others offer a telephone helpline, while others offer no help at all until formal proceedings begin.

If the practitioner finds that he was not insured at the time of the action that has led to the complaint it is too late as far as that particular complaint is concerned but it may be as well to arrange insurance now.

It is also important to get advice from one's professional organization. Should Jaz not belong to a professional organization he may either have to go it alone, which might involve paying for legal advice, or going to the Citizens Advice Bureau and finding out what they can offer and whether he could get legal aid or other assistance.

Many advisers would suggest that the practitioner should respond to the letter in a way that is conciliatory and shows that there is an understanding of what the writer has said. On the other hand, it is important that the practitioner at no stage accepts responsibility for poor professional practice. Such an admission could be used in evidence, should legal proceedings result. This in itself would imply that the practitioner considered himself to be culpable in some way. The analogy here might be with finding yourself in a collision while driving a car. Whether or not you might with hindsight have taken a different course of action, you ought not to jump out of your car and say 'I am sorry, I should have pulled over', thus implying that you should have done something else in the situation.

It might be as well at this point to consider what Joy is wanting from Jaz by writing to him in this way. It is primarily to be and feel heard, it is also to have her 'hurt' acknowledged, and in many cases it is also so that the patient can ensure that others do not experience what she considers to have been insensitive treatment. Therefore Jaz's response to the patient's letter might be to write and say:

> I understand that you felt that the last few sessions have been less than satisfactory from your point of view. I heard this in the last sessions we had together and in your letter. I had felt that your concerns had been discussed in the last session but your letter indicates that you do not feel that the matter has been resolved. I am concerned about this.
>
> Under the circumstances perhaps you would like to have a further session for which I would / would not make any charge so that we can discuss the matter further.
>
> Should you feel that it would be better if this interview took place in the presence of a third party, I would be very willing to ask another colleague to come and meet us both.

First, this letter is conciliatory: it acknowledges the hurt feelings and expresses concern. We are looking for a position to be reached that is comfortable for both parties, but principally for the patient. Jaz can consider with his supervisor what it was in his attitude or practice that has caused the patient to complain, or they may be concerned with Joy's mental processes and what has caused her to make this complaint at this time in the therapy. Joy is caught in her own discomfort and it is from this that she is making the complaint.

Second, the letter opens up the possibility of negotiation and discovery for both parties, if they meet again. They may find out what the original dissatisfaction was about and be able to go on working together; they may decide that the work has reached some sort of impasse and that the patient feels she cannot go forward; or it may be an abortive meeting. But nothing will have been lost. At least an informal conciliation will have been attempted, with the possibility that Joy may feel very much better and that her needs have been attended to.

Third, the letter opens up the possibility of having an independent person present who will observe and might be able to act as a conciliator if that seems to be possible.

Fourth, the practitioner in the letter accepts no liability. There is a fine line between acknowledging feeling and accepting blame. If Jaz has failed in his practice in some way it is unwise to acknowledge this in a letter, as has been said, and doubtless in this case it would have formed part of the discussion in the last session. Confessions of guilt are easily made in trying to be conciliatory and are inappropriate.

In summary, the object of the letter is to acknowledge, to be straightforward and clear, and to treat honestly, to be considerate and not belligerent or defensive.

It is also wise not to be too detailed in any communication, keeping it short and to the point. Above all do not fall into the trap that so many practitioners fall into. Practitioners should not try to reopen the therapy in a letter, making comment and interpretations. Apart from the fact that the situation has changed between the patient and the practitioner, it also reinforces the circumstances that have given rise to the complaint. It may be very important for the patient to see the practitioner as an individual, as another human being rather than her therapist, so that he may be less involved in the transference relationship and all that that involves for a while, allowing the matter to be cleared up.

Let us now consider another example where the writer of the letter of complaint or caller on the telephone is John, the husband of Mary, a patient of Giles. He is accusing Giles of having an affair with his wife because she is so obsessed with him. What might Giles do? Principally, not panic, tread cautiously and respond in a considered manner. It would be important to deny the accusation in a quiet but firm way, and then refer the matter back to the patient, suggesting that John speak to Mary about his concerns and saying that he will need to raise the matter with her himself when they next meet. He would then aim to conclude the call. It is important to be as honest, polite and concise as possible.

Suppose that at this point John becomes abusive and says that he will pursue the matter further. Then it would be best to conclude the call but assume that the matter will not end there.

It would be advisable for Giles to consult his colleagues, remembering, however, that his responsibilities are to his patient and not to a third party. It is important that he bring up the matter with his patient Mary as soon as possible. He should be careful not to fall into blaming John, because John's reactions to what Mary is saying about her therapy could be part of the work Giles needs to do with Mary, understanding the meaning of this particular intrusion into the therapeutic space.

Mary may advise Giles that John will persist. Again this may also be part of the work: she may be someone who has had two people at war over her before. It is important for Giles to keep a professional distance from the situation, on the one hand trying to get on as best he can with the work, while on the other, dealing with a potential professional difficulty. It is important that he should use his consultative support in such a situation. It may be that his professional organization would not consider a complaint from John but it can still be very worrying for the practitioner. Giles might be cited in a divorce case. Always take the best advice available and act in a considered way.

As a practitioner it is important not to underestimate the sense of 'shock' you may experience if you receive a communication of this kind. It is very stressful indeed. However rational your view may be of the value of standards for professional practice and the accountability that goes with membership of a profession, receiving a complaint about one's professional practice is shocking. Within the sense of shock there may also be feelings of outrage, hurt, fear, anger, confusion, fear of exposure, shame and possibly guilt. Again it is not uncommon simply not to know what to do. The need to be rational needs to be managed at the same time as having to manage 'irrational' and quite powerful emotions. However 'innocent' you may feel you are, do not underestimate the stresses and the levels of anxiety that are likely to be provoked.

As a practitioner you will usually be aware of something that has been done or said that has caused the situation to arise, and this can cause you to feel real concern. There may have been a failure of good practice: but, whatever the situation, be sure to take support from colleagues because they will help you to deal with the powerful and contradictory feelings that are part of this process. They will also help you to think: not knowing what to do is a reaction experienced by many who find themselves in these circumstances. So be calm, be patient, think carefully and get others to help you think.

It may be appropriate for the practitioner in such a situation to consider arranging for more supervision or consultative support, or to increase or re-enter personal therapy. This level of support may very well be appropriate. Also it may be a good move to organize around yourself a small support group of those colleagues whom you feel you can trust and who will keep the matter confidential. You might inform your professional organization, if appropriate, and your insurers. If you are in employment you might need to inform your employers and possibly your trade union. You may wish to consult a lawyer, and your insurers may arrange this for you. If so you will be put in touch with a lawyer who has experience in the field.

There are other things that you should do in case the matter is taken further. Keep good notes of any telephone calls, keep letters and copies of responses to them. Then locate all relevant papers, which might include diaries, correspondence, case records, financial accounts, supervision notes and supervision records of your discussions. With them compile and keep a list in date order, it will be invaluable. This could include all appointments and other contacts like telephone calls, letters, postcards sent while on holiday or Christmas cards. It might include significant events that happened during the therapy, outside the therapy like births, or relationships begun or ended within the work. Any absences of yours or the patient's should be recorded, as should any suggestions of the work ending, the actual closure of the work and any subsequent contacts.

If the patient lodges a complaint against you, you will need your chronology. You will also need a record of every action you take, notes of who you sought advice from and records of contacts you have made. You need to keep everything, even if you do not think that it is necessary. It helps you as a practitioner feel that you have a proper control over the problem that besets you.

You may wish to write a history of your training and qualifications, or seek witness testimonials from family, friends and colleagues. The common response is for the practitioner to move into overdrive and generate all sorts of material. This may include detailed descriptions of casework, including other cases. This is not helpful, as it is only the work with the patient concerned that is relevant.

Others move into a position of interpretative analysis and perhaps pathologize the patient. This may help the practitioner's understanding, and, in that the complaint often stems from something that has been said within the session, it is necessary to have a clinical understanding of what is going on. However, practitioners are almost as prone to blaming as patients, and fear breeds impasse, and impasse causes delay. Consultation or supervision of the situation will allow time for reflection on the experience and its likely impact on the rest of the practitioner's casework because of the pressure he is now under.

It is important as the practitioner in this situation to garner your resources and put your energies into the important activities of continuing to run your practice and associated work, and collecting and ordering the relevant material in case a complaint is to be made. Contacting friends and colleagues, apart from those closest who will provide support, may compromise confidentiality. More damage can be done to a counselling or psychotherapy practice by the practitioner telling everyone around about the matter, than by a complaint being pursued, and a misdemeanour being sanctioned by a professional association.

There is also the matter of relevance to the situation. If a patient complains of not being told about paying for missed sessions or holidays taken outside the agreed times, it is not relevant for the practitioner to muster character witnesses. Usually a complaint is about a specific act that the complainant wishes to ensure will not happen again, not about the practitioner's whole practice. So keep a clear focus on the issues under scrutiny and concentrate on evidence relevant to the allegations.

Some practitioners in such a situation find it helpful to keep a separate process record of the impact of the whole experience and the feelings it evokes in them. This needs to be kept completely separate, because it is for the practitioner and their supporters, not for general view.

Let us see how our case studies might be concluded. In the case of Joy, if Jaz responds with the kind of letter outlined above that could be the end of the matter; or there might be a three-way meeting that resolves it; or Joy or Jaz might jointly decide to refer the matter to Jaz's professional organization for them to sort out. If the matter becomes a formal complaint then Jaz would need to prepare a chronology and records of the sessions that Joy was particularly concerned about, as well, perhaps, as making additional notes of his memories of those sessions. He would also need to assemble any consultative or supervisory records from the period that Joy was complaining about, and also since the complaint was made, so that he can be seen to have sought and used appropriate consultative support. Finally he would be keeping a record of any further interactions with Joy from then on.

John's is a different matter: this is a third party complaint, and as such, many professional organizations would not handle it. It could be important for Giles to approach his insurer to find out what legal and financial support might be offered. The complaint is serious, and, if John were to persist in making it, it would need to be handled by a solicitor, because it might be necessary to do something to protect Giles' reputation and stop the spreading of a malicious rumour that could damage his practice.

If, on the other hand, there *are* grounds for John's accusations the professional organization might act on the evidence that John could provide them with. Then Giles might be removed from the professional organization on the grounds that he had brought the profession into disrepute. However, this would be unlikely to happen unless the professional organization already had a considerable and relevant body of knowledge about Giles' activities and John's allegations were the final piece of evidence enabling them to act.

We have seen that if any kind of complaint is made to a practitioner it is most important that he or she seeks advice immediately from his or her supervisor, insurer and professional organization. There should be no admissions of culpability. The practitioner may respond immediately with a brief acknowledgement but then would be wise to wait to make a considered response after consultation with his or her advisers. Many potential complaints have been stopped at this stage through some form of conciliation and both parties have felt satisfied that the matter has been resolved. If however the complaint is pursued, then the practitioner needs to arm him or herself with all possible relevant documentary evidence, as well as the support of colleagues.

# Chapter 8

# Principles for dealing with complaints

In this and the following chapters we will be looking at how an organization might deal with a complaint. Large organizations regularly receive complaints and have a highly complex system to deal with them. For most smaller organizations, however, receiving a complaint is an infrequent occurrence and there may be little expertise available to deal with it. These chapters might be used as a basis for discussion by a large organization, or by smaller organizations as some guidance.

In order to promote public confidence in the profession, any organizational inquisitive or adjudicatory process needs to balance two things, *justice* and *fairness*. Justice and fairness must be ensured both for the person making the complaint and the person who is complained against. Achieving this balance is extremely difficult, but the principle must be constantly borne in mind.

Any organization receiving a complaint needs to consider two further basic principles in dealing with it. The first is *confidentiality*. This is vitally important because patients, who may be making very important accusations, risk being damaged and exposed; practitioners too can find themselves suffering considerable emotional turmoil and loss of earnings through what may turn out to be a complaint by a misguided individual.

When a complaint is received there needs to be a system in place for dealing with it that is completely confidential. This needs to be clearly understood by those who deal with the post and telephone, being the first points of entry. It must then apply throughout the handling of a complaint.

The second principle is the need to *follow complaints procedures with every care*. This is very important for a number of reasons. The complaints procedure explains to the complainant and practitioner in advance how the process will be conducted. They know that when this stage is complete then that will happen within so many days, or if an investigation finds that there have been considerable breaches of codes of ethics then, automatically, adjudication will follow. In other words, the procedures are an element in the matter being dealt with in a fair and just way. They are, in modern parlance, the level playing field which neither party can change. If a case were to end up in the formal judicial system, the Law would be considering whether the procedures were just and had been precisely followed.

If the proper procedure for dealing with a complaint is not followed and breaches of confidentiality take place, justice may not be done. It is the responsibility of the organization to whom the complaint has been made, to protect the complainant so that the complaint can be properly heard and the findings acted upon, while also protecting the member from loss of reputation, professional standing and income as a result of knowledge of the complaint leaking out.

There is always the possibility that the organization may find itself being sued for loss of earnings because a complaint has been made but not proved against a member. The member may be able to show that his business has suffered through the mismanagement of the complaint by the organization. Even if the complaint is proved the member may still be able to sue the organization for loss of earnings if he can show that procedures were not followed or confidentiality not maintained.

## WHO RECEIVES THE COMPLAINT?

In any organization there needs to be a person designated to receive complaints, and administrative staff need to know how to deal with potential complainants. The designated officer may be the chair of the complaints or ethics committee, or may be called the clerk to the committee. This is a very responsible task and would normally fall to the most senior officer of the organization or, in a really large organization, to the second most senior officer, who might well have a legal background. The secretary who services the officers is not appropriate nor is someone who may not stay for long in the job. It must be someone who has a full understanding of and respect for the meaning of confidentiality within a therapeutic setting, and who realizes the necessity of keeping to all the procedures most carefully.

In the first instance a complaint can arrive anywhere in an organization, either in the form of a letter or a telephone call. Administrative staff need to be able to recognize a complaint for what it is and understand how to handle it. For example a person receiving a phone call concerning a complaint needs to be able to take careful notes, while also reacting in a sympathetic way and requesting that the caller put the matter in writing, marked 'confidential', to the person who will deal with it. A letter must also be passed on confidentially, so that it does not land in an 'in tray' where it could be open to the gaze of other members, trainees or even members of the public. The matters referred to in a complaint may be inaccurate or the result of some rumour or misunderstanding, therefore this routing is the first step in what is to become the maintaining of a confidential process throughout.

## WHO MANAGES THE COMPLAINT?

A complaints committee needs to be part of the structure of any therapeutic organization. Its ongoing membership can be small but it needs to have the power to co-opt further members as necessary. It may be useful for the organization to work forwards through the complaints procedure and consider who will be needed if the complaint were to go as far as adjudication and appeal. It is often the chair of the organization who is expected, either alone or with an outside person, to hear an appeal. This is particularly important because any member can only be involved at one stage, at a hearing or at appeal. If a two-stage process is to be used, three senior members may be needed to adjudicate; and they should include at least one member of the ethics committee. So the initial processes of investigation and mediation may need to be carried out by another member of the committee accompanied by another senior member of the organization. Anyone cited in a complaint or anyone who would be considered to be personally or therapeutically associated with him or her should not be part of the complaints committee nor take part in disciplinary hearings.

An appropriate complaints committee for a small association might have three members, one of whom would be the chair. A common problem can arise when a complaint is received by the chair of the complaints committee and one of the two other members of the committee is either the therapist or supervisor of the practitioner complained against or the complainant's therapist or supervisor. The therapist or supervisor concerned cannot be involved in the investigation, and at this stage a third person who is independent of the complainant must be co-opted to consider the case. In other words it is of primary importance that anyone who might be concerned with either the complainant or the person complained against is kept free of the complaints process. If this is not adhered to, complaints material may infect other processes of the organization: information from the complaint could get into therapy, or information from therapy or supervision into the complaint.

All the way through the processing of a complaint the people chosen by the complaints committee to handle the matter need to be respected and trusted members of the organization. It is usual to include those who have relevant experience and also the 'grand old' women and men of the organization. This may seem to be all very well, but standards change and many things that were perfectly acceptable say fifteen years ago are no longer considered good practice today. Thus any group needs to include people who have an up-to-date understanding of good practice issues. Public confidence in the process can be increased by involving a person of standing from outside the organization as a 'lay representative'.

The choice of personnel is often far easier for the large organization where the overlapping knowledge or experience between one member and another is likely to be far less. In such organizations there may be a standing complaints committee which gathers considerable experience of managing complaints during the members' terms of office. They are often less likely to be taken over by the emotion of a situation and able to bring a parity of treatment to a broad range of cases.

In order to help ensure that the complaints procedure is strictly followed, the process needs to be as simple as possible. It should include protocols for all meetings that might take place, in other words, outline structures of the meetings, how time needs to be allocated and what progress or outcome is expected from each meeting.

## IS IT A COMPLAINT OR A MATTER FOR A HEALTH COMMITTEE?

Some matters which are presented to a complaints committee are immediately identifiable as relating to the health of the practitioner. Since many practitioners work well beyond the conventional retirement age, cases occur which are to do with the practitioner's health and may, in the interests of justice and fairness, be better attended to, as they would be in the medical world, by a health committee. This committee could be formed in a similar way to a complaints committee but it considers whether the health of the practitioner in some way limits his or her performance.

Let us look at a complaint against an elderly and respected psychotherapist, John Smith,who has recently been falling asleep and is unable to follow the course of a supervision session for his supervisee Anna.

Anna may be concerned that her letter of complaint might damage her chances of qualification, because John Smith is very well thought of by both his own organization and the one Anna is training with, yet she is equally concerned that if she does nothing she will not have had adequate supervision to write her qualifying paper.

The supervisee, we hope, will already have exhausted other modes of negotiation. She will have spoken to John directly, and although John mentioned not being well recently he has not take on board Anna's repeated complaints. Anna may have spoken to a member of John's organization and to the chair of their professional committee or the person responsible for the training. As likely as not, they will each have referred her back to her supervisor, John. This is the kind of vicious circle that, though good practice, may cause clients, trainees and supervisees great frustration. In many cases the supervisee would give up and move to another supervisor if this were open to her, feeling that the buck is constantly being passed. Anna is, however, persistent and feels she must make a complaint because she will not be allowed to change supervisors for her training patient and she wants attention to be given to the situation.

Her complaint should be picked up as a potential health matter and may be dealt with by an informal meeting. This meeting will give Anna the sense that she is being heard and that the matter of the elderly practitioner is clearly in the hands of the organization, and she may be satisfied. In meeting the supervisor, the members may be surprised to discover the state of ill-health of their colleague and advise him that he should consider reducing his workload and responsibilities to clients, trainees and supervisees. The practitioner may not be willing to do so, feeling that he is in perfectly good enough health to manage his present workload. Here we have another kind of impasse and it will become a matter for the health committee to pursue with the professional organization. They will become the maintainers of standards and advise the ruling body of the organization what they feel should be done.

## THE MANAGEMENT OF THE COMPLAINT

First let us consider how the papers which will be copied and circulated during the management of a complaint are to be dealt with. In order to ensure confidentiality it may be best not to do this in an office within the organization. It may be that the organization's trusted secretary will become part of the team who are dealing with the complaint, and that the physical management of the complaint is done in another place such as his or her home or the home of the chair of the complaints committee. Even so confidentiality may be compromised, if for instance, photo-copying has to be done at a copy shop where a vital page might be left in the photocopier.

Second there is the question of how the hearings will be recorded. It is important that both complainant and complained against have a record of what questions they have been asked and what they have said at a hearing. As a result it has become usual for the proceedings to be recorded either on tape or by shorthand. Recording can be managed effectively on fairly simple machinery as long as it can pick up voices from all parts of the room. Since the practical skills of many therapists are wanting, it may be wise to have a back-up machine, and make a second tape recording as well. Some sections of the therapeutic profession are quite used to working with tape recorders but others are not and may not wish to have the equipment there. The alternative, which is very much more expensive and could compromise confi-dentiality, is to hire a secretary who can take verbatim shorthand, which can then be transcribed into a full report. An accurate, complete record of the meeting is very important for future meetings, appeals and other proceedings which could follow. Note-taking is not sufficient.

## SUPPORT FOR THOSE WHO ARE INVOLVED IN DEALING WITH A COMPLAINT

Almost everyone who is involved in a complaint needs some support during the process. The complainant may be under considerable strain, as it often takes a great deal of courage to make a complaint. The strain and anxiety caused to the practitioner who is complained against cannot be underestimated, and he or she may very well need to find support through supervision, consultation or therapy.

Those who carry out investigations or adjudications also feel considerably burdened by the information they hear and the feelings they receive at a hearing. What should they do? Consultation may be appro-priate, but this enlarges the group that need to hold the confidentiality. Sometimes the group feel that they can support one another. Often, however, their feelings are most properly noted down to be put in a separate short process report for the complaints committee only. Such a report is inclined to contain the subjective material that there is no room for, nor is it appropriate that there should be, in the objective report produced for the complaints committee.

This is an ongoing theme in complaints work: the need and demand is always for objective reporting, while psychotherapists and counsellors work in a subjective world. Complaints panels may find therefore that writing objective reports can leave them with complex feelings which also need an appropriate outlet.

We have seen that the powerful feelings arising on both sides of complaints, and the delicate and potentially damaging material they concern, make the maintenance of confidentiality vital. It is essential too that organizations should have clear procedures in place so that complaints can be dealt with from the start in a calm, efficient and fair manner.

# Chapter 9

# Putting complaints procedures into practice

In the next four chapters we will look at what a complaints procedure consists of and how it will work in practice. We will follow three complaints that might come into an organization and see how they might be dealt with.

The first case begins when Rose, a patient, telephones an organization to say that she has just been to a lecture by her past therapist, Ray, and has recognized that he was using her case material. Although names were changed in the lecture, both her partner and a colleague who was with her had recognized that the case material was Rose's. Rose is particularly distressed because details were mentioned that she had chosen not to tell either her colleague or her partner.

The secretary receiving this call immediately recognizes the complaint as being about a breach of confidentiality and therefore an ethical matter. She asks Rose to telephone the chair of the ethics or complaints committee, who then asks Rose to put her complaint in writing.

The second complainant is David, who has been a twice-weekly patient of Barbara's for three years. David feels that his therapy is going nowhere and that Barbara is particularly caught up with his pre-birth and neonate experiences, while he is concerned about what is happening at work in his very high-powered job. David writes directly to the chair of the complaints committee after having telephoned to inquire about the procedure in that particular organization.

The third complaint comes from Sue, who was in counselling with Trevor for five years until two years ago when she stopped her therapy after a brief affair with him ended. She has just met another former patient of Trevor's, Jane, and realized that Jane has also been his lover. Jane in turn knows of two other women in the same position. Although Jane is unwilling to complain, Sue feels strongly enough to make a formal complaint and she telephones the umbrella organization asking how she can do this.

## THE FORMULATION OF THE COMPLAINT

There are inclined to be confused feelings mixed with incoherent facts in the first statements made in a complaint. But it is vital that the complainant should make a clear statement about his or her perceived injury. If the complaint is serious but not clearly formulated, then the matter can be hard to manage, since the meaning of the complaint can be interpreted in different ways and may metamorphose during the processing.

It is often helpful if the complainant uses the code of ethics and practice of the organization or the ethical guidelines of the umbrella organization as the basis of formulating the complaint. The code can work as a template or guide and help to clarify and order feelings and thoughts about the cause of complaint. Once the complainant has read a code and decided what he or she wants to say there can be a completely different feel to the importance of the communication.

Rose might decide to make her complaint by stating that the matter is a breach of confidentiality, while also claiming professional misconduct. It seems that Ray assumed he was safe to divulge her material believing her to be out of the country. Rose also states that she does not wish anyone but the members of the complaints committee to know that she is making a complaint. She is now in another therapy and training as a psychotherapist and she wants to be sure that Ray does not use her material again and above all does not publish it.

Sue, in her complaint against Trevor, might decide to quote the clause in the code of ethics and practice that refers to gross professional misconduct, or which refers to exploiting patients emotionally and sexually.

The purpose of getting the complaint written down and related to a code is so that it is fixed and the complaints committee can consider what should happen about it. Also, as a matter of natural justice, the practitioner has the right to know exactly what misconduct is alleged against him or her.

## THE ACKNOWLEDGEMENT OF THE COMPLAINT

When a properly formulated complaint is received by the chair of the committee or clerk it needs to be acknowledged immediately in writing.

*It is a fundamental matter of good practice in dealing with complaints, that all communications are acknowledged as soon as possible.* The acknowledgement may not contain any reply, but it is useful if it does say when a reply might be expected. It is also important that during the whole progress of the complaint, complainant and practitioner are kept fully informed about what is happening.

The complaints committee needs to be convened to decide whether the complaint is properly formulated, whether there may have been a breach of the codes of ethics and practice and thus whether there is a complaint to answer.

Should the complaint not be satisfactorily formulated the committee will need to decide what advice or assistance it wishes to give the complainant. It is important that the complainant is given a fair chance to express him or herself. It is not good enough for the complaints committee to keep returning a poorly formulated complaint to the complainant on the grounds of inadequate formulation. It may be necessary for one of their own members to act as an advocate and work with the complainant to help him or her clarify the issues involved and formulate the complaint. Or the committee might encourage the complainant to get independent help through formal or informal advocacy, say from a Citizens Advice Bureau.

In the cases of Rose and Sue the complaints committee will have been able clearly to detect the cause of complaint. However, in David's case, the grounds for complaint may be less clear. In the end he might formulate it by citing clauses of a code of practice which address contract making and the stating of qualifications by the practitioner.

Sometimes it is obvious that the complainant 'wants' something and that is the reason they give for making the complaint. The committee may need to inform the complainant if what they want could not, in any circumstances, be an outcome of the complaint. For instance, the complainant may be asking for the return of a year's fees paid to the practitioner for sessions she attended or may want to have personal information which it would be inappropriate for her to have. These are not matters within the jurisdiction of the complaints committee and the complainant needs to know this.

## ACCEPTING THE COMPLAINT

If the complaints committee accepts that there may be grounds for complaint then some form of investigation will be needed. The chair of the committee needs to write to both parties and inform them that a complaint has been made and accepted and that the committee has decided that there will be an *informal procedure*, possibly followed by a *formal procedure*. Both parties need to be clearly advised that they should preserve confidentiality. The ring of confidentiality must be maintained and it is the responsibility of all parties to do this.

It is understood that both complainant and the practitioner complained against will need support during the processing of the complaint. For the practitioner this should come from the supervisor, consultant and a peer group, while the complainant might be advised to form a small group of friends or colleagues who might support them. All parties need to be apprised of the importance of maintaining confidentiality and the consequences if it is breached. If the complainant speaks openly about the matter and it becomes general knowledge, it is usual for the complaint to be dropped. If the practitioner breaks confidentiality then this breach, in itself, could be a matter for sanction by the professional organization.

## THE INFORMAL PROCEDURE

Many organizations like to have the possibility of an informal process built into their complaints procedure and may choose to use it before the complaint becomes fixed. This is quite legitimate. Informal processes work well where there are cases of therapeutic impasse of some sort or another.

In an informal process it is usual for one or two people to meet with the complainant and the practitioner, often, in the first case, separately and then together, as long as the procedures allow for it. If the complaints committee can develop its skills of mediation and negotiation many potential complaints can be resolved at an informal stage.

The case between David and Barbara might be managed like this. The committee might feel that, in David's case, a colleague who is completely impartial should speak to David and Barbara, to try to discover if there is really a cause for complaint or whether the complaint comes from a particularly painful or negative part of their work. Let us say that they both meet Joe, an analyst known for his experience in conciliation.

It may transpire that David had been told clearly about the nature of the therapy he was to receive and had even been given a pamphlet by Barbara, explaining her method of working, at their first meeting. This also had the initials of her qualifications after her name. It may also have been that David was so upset and frightened that he took in nothing of their first meeting and subsequently left his briefcase on the bus. Joe might help them both tell their experience of what happened to one another and the matter might be resolved.

On the other hand it may have been that Barbara did not explain anything to David at their first meeting, that she moved immediately into a therapeutic stance and analysed all future inquiries as part of the transference. David has complained out of his frustration at this. In these circumstances Joe might recommend that the complaint should be accepted because he believes that Barbara failed to make an adequate contract.

An informal intervention can be timely and can resolve a therapeutic impasse for the patient. In some cases the work may then be resumed. However, the informal meeting will doubtless cause considerable work for the therapy. Both patient and practitioner need to understand the meaning of David's wish to complain.

## THE FORMAL PROCEDURE

The complaints committee must be careful that by using an informal procedure it is not stifling the legitimate and serious concerns of complainants. If there is a proper complaint backed up by clear and good evidence, it should be heard. An informal process should not be used to get a member of an organization or complaints committee out of difficulty, for instance when a well-known or senior practitioner who is capable of putting a lot of pressure on the committee challenges their authority. If there is a case to be answered it needs to be heard. In small organizations where virtually every member will be known to the members of the complaints committee, the committee may come under considerable pressure to manage complaints outside the official procedures.

It would be inappropriate to use an informal process in the cases of between Rose and Ray or between Sue and Trevor, since there are substantive issues in both cases. There is also additional corroborative evidence, which might include the statements of others about Ray's lecture, or in the case of Sue, the similar experiences of other female patients.

The formal process begins when the complaints committee accepts the complaint and decides to follow the formal procedure. The principles that the members will be keeping in mind are those of fairness and justice in each situation. They also need to maintain confidentiality and keep to their own procedures. Their consideration must be that right is seen to be done by the purchaser of the service, the supervisee, trainee or client. Protection must also be given to the practitioner, the member complained against.

## PROCEEDING WITH A COMPLAINT

In accepting a complaint, the committee needs to know what it is going to do about it, and how it will be progressed. If the basis of the complaint is known to the committee and the matter is serious, the committee may decide that it would be appropriate to begin with an investigatory process. Alternatively it might decide to use a process that could also be adjudicatory, in other words, it may embark on either a two-stage or a single-stage process.

## CHOOSING THE MOST APPROPRIATE COMPLAINTS PROCESS

Complaints procedures may involve one, two or three formal stages. Each of these systems has advantages and disadvantages.

| Single-stage | Two-stage | Three-stage |
| --- | --- | --- |
| Investigation with Adjudication | Investigation with one or two investigators + Adjudication | Investigation + Conciliation + Adjudication |

A three-stage process involves separate investigation, mediation and adjudication. In my experience this does not work. If a complaint becomes formal then mediation or conciliation are no longer possible. Decisions are wanted and needed. The three-stage procedure is over-long, involves too many people, is an unnecessary strain on all concerned and an unnecessary expense for the organization.

There is now considerable use of a two-stage process of investigation followed by adjudication. Previously it was believed that a more prolonged procedure was helpful to those involved, but experience shows that both parties want matters resolved speedily. Unless the matter of complaint is particularly complex or unclear, a one-stage process is quite adequate. One of the difficulties with a two-stage process is that if either party gets a sense from an investigation that the matter is not going his or her way, he or she can be very obstructive and hard to handle, particularly after receiving the investigation report and when making arrangements for the subsequent meetings.

In devising procedures it is important to consider the size of the organization. In larger organizations within the BAC, the BCP, the BPS and the UKCP two-stage and three-stage processes are used and those who hear the case do not know the parties to the complaint. The complaint itself is normally clearly formulated before it comes to the complaints committee, having been thoroughly reviewed by the clerk. In such circumstances, it can be argued that a double process can allow plenty of time for the gathering of information. However, in many cases all the information may be available right from the beginning and there can be a sense of wasting time in investigating something that everyone knows must be adjudicated.

Increasingly there is a conviction that single-stage processes come up with just and fair outcomes, even in organizations of some considerable size. Smaller organizations can only provide the personnel for a single-stage complaints procedure. Here the practitioner, against whom the complaint is being made, will be a peer of those hearing the case and necessarily known to them, and there are not enough personnel to manage a lengthy complaint without confidentiality being stretched beyond its limits and the practitioner's career within the organization potentially being damaged. There can also be considerable difficulties within smaller organizations, managing a complaint which touches two or more members. For example when the complainant sees the practitioner's consultant or supervisor as being partly responsible since he or she was overseeing the clinical work of the practitioner, or the chair of the organization as responsible because, when the complainant consulted him or her, there was a delay in sending a copy of the codes and complaints procedure of the organization. Then a multiple complaint can ensue, stretching the organization's qualified personnel to its limit.

With a single-stage process the matter can be dealt with expeditiously. The strain on the organization and on the parties concerned is less. The outcomes can be sound and both complainant and practitioner have the backstop of appeal.

The complaints committee might decide to deal with the case of Sue and Trevor by a single-stage process because the evidence submitted is clear and there are clear supporting statements. They might also decide to consider Rose and Ray's case in a similar way. However, if the evidence is unclear, they might opt to investigate first. They might argue that David's case against Barbara warranted investigation since they would hope to stop it there and avoid the need for adjudication.

We have seen that it is essential for a complainant to formulate a complaint clearly, defining which aspect of the codes of ethics and practice a practitioner is alleged to have breached. The complaints committee will then be able to assess the seriousness of the complaint, and whether it can best be dealt with by an informal or a formal process. In all cases the need to resolve the matter as simply and swiftly as possible must be balanced against the need for thoroughness and the following of procedures.

# Chapter 10

# Investigation

The purpose of an investigation is to decide if there is 'a case to answer':
whether the facts of the complaint, if proved, would potentially amount
to misconduct and whether or not there is sufficient information available to warrant proceeding to an adjudication. In a two-stage process
the investigation is normally a fairly informal meeting where the investigator or investigators look at the evidence submitted and speak to both
parties about the allegations made in the complaint.

It is usual to have a single investigator who will work alongside the
clerk to the committee or a committee member who will attend so that he
or she can assist, manage the event, monitor the proceedings and see that
the procedure and protocols for the meeting are followed. However,
sometimes the complainant or member complained against may be
particularly vociferous, angry or powerful, and a single investigator may
not feel able to manage the situation. Under such circumstances, it is
wise to have a second investigator so that one can be asking questions
while the other monitors the process. They may choose to take turns in
these roles.

A protocol must be issued before the meeting, setting out the order
of the proceedings and the amount of time that should be given to each
party. The principles that should govern the meeting are those of natural
justice: first the proceedings should be *just and fair*, for example equal
time needs to be given to both parties. Second it is important to ensure
the *protection and safety of both parties*. Both of these principles need to
be clearly kept in mind.

In the case of Rose, having complained about her ex-therapist who
is a well-known lecturer, she may feel fearful of challenging such a
person. She may feel that she does not wish to meet Ray at all during the
progress of the complaint. In a two-stage process she need not meet
him at the investigation but she would be expected to meet him at

adjudication. However, if there are exceptional circumstances, a special protocol might be considered. There is a parallel in law courts where, in some cases of severe abuse or rape, television monitors are used so that individuals can be questioned apart and the complainant and alleged perpetrator do not meet. The rarity of this happening in judicial cases should be a guide to those who manage the quasi-legal processes of complaints procedures.

A protocol may include guidance on what the investigators will consider acceptable in the way of evidence; when it should be submitted by; whether new evidence will be acceptable at the hearing itself and, if so, in what form; and whether evidence is available to all parties. It is helpful for the investigators to have full, written submissions well before the hearing. The complaint will have been served on the practitioner, the complainant will have provided corroborating evidence and the practitioner will need to have responded, as clearly as possible, on all the breaches of the codes the complainant cites. All these papers should be submitted by a fixed date before the investigatory hearing so that they may be copied and sent out to both parties and the investigator. The evidence needs to be as complete as possible so that the questions the investigator asks can be as informed and pertinent as possible.

The question of whether evidence should be made available to all parties is often a contentious one. The rule used at tribunals, which is the nearest formal comparison to a complaints procedure, is that it should. Practitioners often feel concerned by this since they feel that their defence lies within the relationship they have had with the patient, namely in the transference relationship. They do not want to submit written evidence which concerns clinical judgement in case it is misunderstood or misused. This is a complex area and certainly at an investigatory stage it may be more appropriate for such material to form part of the discussion between the investigator and the practitioner alone. However, it is increasingly accepted within the profession, as well as by the world at large, that all matters to do with complaints are open. This follows what is accepted as good practice in terms of equal opportunities and public accountability.

The protocol may also offer guidance on what conduct the investigators will consider acceptable. This might include: advice to all parties regarding confidentiality; advice about and any sanctions in the case of prejudicial statements or behaviour; what will be considered unacceptable behaviour by any party and what will be done about it.

We have discussed at length the need for confidentiality in all matters that concern complaints. However, it is possible that at the investigation stage, new people will enter the ring of confidentiality. They may be supporters of the complainant, or the supervisor or consultant of the practitioner. Whoever they are they must be apprised of the need for confidentiality. One of the reasons for this is that breaches of confidentiality can be prejudicial to the outcome of the complaint. In a small community knowledge that a complaint is in progress can put pressure on either party or their supporters and cause a legitimate complaint to be withdrawn or a complainant to feel that he or she has been harmed. It can also cause other professionals, possibly those who might be involved in adjudication, to feel influenced.

In some cases a problem that threatens to prejudice the management and outcome of the complaint can come from the distressed behaviour of the complainant or practitioner. He or she may telephone or write repeatedly, may be rude, even very rude, when the process is being managed in the best possible way. Such aggressive behaviour is not uncommon from complainants, but also, perhaps less expectedly, from practitioners. We all understand that both feel very disturbed and distressed; but aggressive and disrespectful behaviour helps no one. It may be that the organization should limit contact with whichever party is causing difficulty. It may have to consider how much rudeness it will accept from the member before sanction.

Complainants can be equally badly behaved, but tight boundaries and speedy processing of the complaint, keeping both parties well informed by letter and aware of timings and meetings, can help considerably. The committee can request that the complainant behaves in a reasonable manner.

Once the papers have been sent out, all the parties including the investigator or investigators need time to consider them. Should the investigator be working alone, he or she may wish to talk the matter over with a consultant, perhaps his or her own consultant for clinical work, another member of the organization or someone outside the organization who is an expert in organizational matters or complaints work. In all cases this should have been agreed with the complaints committee. If there are two investigators they may wish to meet before the hearing. If they are at a distance they may decide to work on the telephone and then meet before the formal meeting. They need to discuss the issues that the papers raise and consider the questions that they wish to ask.

In the case of Rose and Ray they will want clear evidence of what was said at the lecture and may ask both Rose and Ray if they can provide it. They will also want corroborative statements from Rose's partner and colleague and from Ray. From Barbara they will want copies of her pamphlet and any other information that she provides for patients. In the case of Sue and Trevor they will want the clearest statements possible from all concerned.

It is helpful for the investigators to prepare a history of the actions that have led to the complaint. This will be very similar to the chronology that it has been previously suggested the practitioner compiles. It may be drawn from the practitioner's notes and from the evidence provided by the complainant before and during the investigation. Investigators who do this before the hearing find themselves better orientated in relation to the material before them. They can discover discrepancies in timing or variations in the order of events recorded by one party or the other. These can often be very pertinent to the misunderstandings that have given rise to the complaint and may give a clear guide to questioning.

It may be that Trevor's dates for the completion of therapy are at variance with Sue's, and the investigators may request that Sue provide evidence from diaries and dated bills.

The investigators will need to decide which are the serious issues that have been raised by the complainant, but also to attend to all the issues that have been raised because it is important for all the aspects of the complaint to be considered. The investigators may need to monitor their own feelings so that they do not get over-involved in some particular concern and become fixed on one issue or point of view. There are clear parallels with the therapeutic process here, and as with clinical work so with complaints, it is necessary to be involved in the process while also observing it.

An investigation of this kind is a formal hearing and needs to take place in a formal setting such as the offices of the organization concerned. Should this not provide the confidentiality necessary then a neutral setting elsewhere should be used.

The person or people who are monitoring the meeting, the clerk or members of the complaints committee, have three roles: they are the stage managers of the occasion, seeing that things happen on time and in the right way according to the protocol; they are the holders of the knowledge as far as the procedure is concerned and must keep it on course; they also watch what is going on and advise if the questioning is becoming one-sided or in any other way might prejudice a fair outcome.

Rose might say that she was in therapy with Ray Brown for four years, and that during the therapy she spoke about being physically assaulted as a child. At the lecture Rose had recognized her own case material, which was particularly identifiable because she was beaten with a riding crop and this was mentioned. She feels that Ray had hardly disguised her story at all. She adds that when she ended her therapy with Ray she went to live in New Zealand with her fiancé but she has now been back in the United Kingdom for three years. Rose, in other words, fills out the evidence of her original letter of complaint of breaches of confidentiality. The fact that Ray spoke in public about her clinical material without seeking her permission and did so in a way that made her easily recognizable to her colleagues and others, has broken her confidence and caused her professional embarrassment. She also says that Ray behaved unprofessionally and carelessly since he clearly assumed that Rose was still living in New Zealand. Rose also feels that the lecture involved public statements about her physical abuse that were over-emphasized and voyeuristic.

As far as the investigators are concerned, in considering this very serious breach of confidence, they may wish to have a copy of the paper presented, and might ask if the lecture was taped, since speakers often divert from their text. This evidence needs to be obtained before the investigation meeting so that the investigator's questioning can be fully pertinent.

The investigators need to use the time of the meeting to establish from Rose and anyone else she may choose to bring, for example her partner and colleague, what was said that led them to realize that Ray was speaking about her personal material. They then need to question Ray about his case material and try to gain some sense of his attitude to the material he presented.

Ray might say that the case material was not Rose's at all but belonged to another patient; or he might agree that it was her material and plead that he did not know how to contact her; or he might claim that he sought her permission in his initial contract with her when she began therapy with him some eight years ago.

When both Rose and Ray have been interviewed, the investigators will need time to consider whether the case made by the complainant Rose is sound and there is likely to have been a breach of ethical or practice codes. If they believe that there has been a breach the case must go forward to adjudication however sympathetic the investigators may feel towards the practitioner.

If Ray says that the case material was based on quite another case and the matter is very unclear and seems to have more to do with the ending of the therapy and the two personalities in some therapeutic impasse, the task of the investigators is more complex because they are going to have to decide whether there was or was not a breach.

The experience of investigators is often that they feel totally persuaded by the complainant and then totally persuaded by the practitioner. The dynamics of splitting that lie behind this kind of experience are known. It is therefore advisable that those who hear investigations take plenty of time to consider each stage of the meeting, hold an impartial stance and use the possibility of questioning each party more than once if they wish to.

This could be so in the case of Sue and Trevor. Sue might first give a very distressing account of her relationship with Trevor. Then when Jane's statement is tabled, it is ill-written and almost illiterate, irritating the investigator. Trevor then presents himself as a very competent professional, in suit and tie, and uses all his charm, claiming that he has been misunderstood and that Sue and Jane are in the grip of fantasies: they are distressed women who find him attractive. The investigator needs to be able to give credence to Sue's distress, see Jane's contribution as the product of limited education and her own distress, and see behind Trevor's presentation, to discern what may really be going on.

When the investigation is complete, and those investigating feel that they are in command of the facts, a report will need to be written. Whether the investigation is likely to close the matter or whether the investigator suggests that there may be a case to answer, the facts and argument followed by the investigator need to be clearly reported in order to inform the ensuing discussion by the complaints committee. The report will become a fundamental part of any information presented at adjudication.

## MEDIATION

During an investigation it may sometimes seem that the complaint can be resolved by mediation. The complainant often states that he or she only wants an apology. However, if the apology is offered, the complainant may begin to make a series of demands of the practitioner which are unacceptable to him or her or the insurers, and perhaps also unacceptable to the organization concerned.

There is rarely room for mediation in a complaints matter. If a complaint has been formalized it has normally become fixed, and the parties concerned are already too involved in their own feelings and anger towards one another to resolve the matter in this way. So if mediation is suggested it needs to take place on grounds which are clearly stated, written down and agreed in advance. It is best handled by a well-briefed third party, someone who knows the outcome of the investigation but who is able to help both parties to find a way forward.

My experience is that every mediatory process held at this stage of a complaints procedure has broken down because the issues that seem to have been resolved suddenly mutate and an impasse ensues. The manner in which this happens is in parallel process to the complaint. The dynamic processes are acted out as soon as the formal containment of the investigative structure and complaints procedure is removed. Containment is only regained when the procedure is re-established. The procedure can provide containment as safe and sure as psychotherapy itself. Mediation is best confined to the preliminary informal process, not introduced at the later, formal stage.

## THE INVESTIGATION REPORT

The purpose of the investigation report is to clarify the facts for the complaints committee and help them decide whether the case should progress to the next stage. It is an informative summary and also becomes part of 'the evidence' at the next stage. An investigation report needs to include two main sections. The first will include the history of the actions that have led to the complaint, which was probably prepared before the investigation itself. This can be filled out with information obtained during the hearing.

The second part addresses each cause of complaint or each clause of the codes or ethics and practice cited by the complainant. Areas of agreement and disagreement are then enumerated in relation to each cause or clause. The investigator then addresses the evidence for and against the breaching of each clause of the code or each cause of complaint. He or she needs to be clear about the facts and their findings. It is often very hard for psychotherapists and counsellors to think in terms of facts; they are far more used to subjective rather than objective reporting. Then the investigator states on each count whether there may be a case for adjudication. This report is advisory, not prescriptive.

The report is being prepared for the complaints committee, but a copy of it will go to both the complainant and the practitioner against whom the complaint has been made. Both will need to be given the opportunity to respond.

The report on Rose and Ray may say that, in the view of the investigator, Rose gave clear evidence and Ray was nonchalant, not taking the cause of complaint or the process at all seriously. Ray might challenge this and provide a printed text and clarification of what he said. Rose would probably say little, since the report supported her point of view. The report on Sue and Trevor may say that Sue and Jane were not convincing witnesses and Trevor showed himself as a true professional. Sue might well respond with clarifications, further evidence and sworn affidavits.

It is usual for there to be some challenge to details and interpretations of the facts by both parties at this stage. If either party is unsatisfied with the fair-mindedness of the investigation, he or she will pursue the complaint further or claim that his or her professional reputation has been damaged by the mishandling of the investigation by a colleague.

The report needs to be written within the stated amount of time after the meeting, as set out by the complaints procedure. Five or ten working days are usually adequate. The longer the investigators have to write the report the greater the difficulty they often experience in writing it. The detail is easily forgotten and they then need to remind themselves of what was said. However, colleagues who may be working for the organization on a voluntary or semi-voluntary basis need to be given adequate time to manage their regular commitments also. Delay will cause distress to the parties concerned.

The complaints committee needs to consider the report alongside any responses received from the parties concerned; there may be errors that can be corrected. The information should then be as complete as possible for the adjudicatory process. Circulating the report in this way helps to keep the procedures as transparent as possible for all those who are party to the proceedings. If reports are not made available they are the subject of fantasies and the parties are likely to suspect the integrity of the investigators and complaints committee. Occasionally there are issues that are confidential to one or other side in an inquiry, and as a result it may be necessary to have a section or sections that are separate and only go to the party concerned. It is essential that the investigators and complaints committee consider why they are doing this, because it may well reflect the dynamics of the complaint. There are certainly occasions when, for the safety of one party or other, it would be both unfortunate and inappropriate for a complete report to be given to one party. This is particularly so where the report might be used against the practitioner in a civil action in the courts.

# THE DELIBERATIONS OF THE COMPLAINTS COMMITTEE

In the discussion of the investigator's report the complaints committee considers whether: the task of investigation has been carried out in a satisfactory manner; the report is full enough; the recommendations of the report are sound; and what further action needs to be taken.

The complaints committee is responsible for the investigation: it has commissioned it and is ultimately responsible to the organization for it. Therefore, it needs to be satisfied that the task has been carried out in a just and fair manner and according to the procedures laid down by the organization. The members of the committee then need to consider if the report has been properly compiled, and whether they are satisfied with the evidence provided on each count. They will need to consider the additional comments that the complainant and practitioner may have made in response to the report, and if these make substantive differences to the case, how this might affect their decision. They now need to decide whether any further information needs to be sought.

In the light of the information that they now have they need to decide whether to accept the investigator's report. The complaints committee used the investigator or investigators as its agents and would need to show good reason to disagree with them.

The investigators may advise, in the case of Rose and Ray and Sue and Trevor, that there clearly is a matter for adjudication on the evidence presented to them. In accepting their report the committee needs to decide how to move forward. It will need to consider each cause of complaint or clause of the codes, depending on how the complaint was made and investigation heard. Then it will consider whether to stop the procedure and end the matter; or to adjudicate the case on some grounds but perhaps not on others; or to adjudicate the whole matter.

# Chapter 11

# Adjudication

An adjudication is the part of the proceedings when all the available evidence will be heard and the adjudicators will decide on their view of the matter. An adjudication may be a separate meeting following an investigation or, in a single-stage process, it is one part of the combined meeting. The single-stage process is most appropriate where the evidence is considerable and clear, or where the practitioner acknowledges that the complainant's accusation is valid. It also suits a smaller organization where any difficulties need to be dealt with quickly and where there are relatively few people to manage complaints.

## THE VENUE FOR THE MEETING

An adjudication can in some ways be compared to a tribunal. It is a formal meeting and therefore requires a formal setting. A suitable venue might be the main room of the offices of the organization. If this does not provide the necessary privacy then a neutral setting may be needed elsewhere, such as rooms at a hotel or at a local voluntary or learned society. The atmosphere and environment need to be formal, but informal space is needed nearby where people can wait.

## THE PANEL

The people who are chosen to form an adjudication panel need to be people of stature within the organization. The procedures and the way in which they are managed can be questioned at any stage through judicial review, which, in English law, is an action of the High Court to review the decision of a lower court, tribunal or administrative body. Therefore, the organization needs to be seen to be behaving responsibly. The complaints committee must ensure when selecting a panel that they represent the interests of both parties. In the cases of Rose and Ray, Sue and Trevor and David and Barbara there should be a man and a woman on the panel. Should one of the parties come from a minority community it is important to have a representative from that community. The panel might need to consider the socio-economic background, sexual orientation and age also: all parties need representation in terms of equal opportunities. It may be particularly useful to include a person from outside the organization in order to represent an independent view on the panel.

When asking people to join the panel, the complaints committee need to be sure that those they approach are independent of the complaint and have never been the therapist or supervisor of the practitioner, because, in asking them to join, they will be revealing the names of the parties to the complaint. Should anyone approached feel that he or she needs to declare an interest or could be compromised by being part of the panel, he or she should say so before learning any more about the matter. The names should also be checked with the parties to the complaint because they may have a reasonable objection to a particular person being asked to join the panel. It could be that someone who is approached was in the same training group as one of the parties, or they may have worked in the same clinic, or may have sat on committees together, and this might feel very compromising. After the opinions of the parties have been sought the panel is constituted. It now needs a chair. Often the complaints committee will have chosen a particular person to be on the panel because of his or her abilities in chairing meetings and tribunals and in this case the committee should decide on the chair themselves. If not, it will be the first task of the constituted panel to appoint their chair.

## THE MEETING DATE

A meeting date then needs to be agreed. The complaints committee will need to decide how flexible it is willing to be. It may offer three dates convenient to the panel and still not get agreement from the parties.The practitioner can to some extent be pressured to attend at the panel's convenience, but the complainant may be restricted by reasonable work commitments, and may or may not be willing to travel. The committee will need to take a view about what level of expenses it should meet. The party who feels more disadvantaged by the complaint is often the more difficult to fix a date with, and the excuses for cancelling meetings or refusing to fix dates can be legion and most inventive. Once a date is agreed it needs to be put in writing to all the parties concerned and confirmation sought in writing by return.

## A 'FRIEND' OR SUPPORTER

At an adjudicatory meeting it is usual for the persons appearing to bring a 'friend' or person to support them. This might be a colleague, or it could be a legal adviser. Legal representatives, such as solicitors, at hearings cause the procedure to become more confrontational and often more complicated. However the practitioner is trying to protect his or her livelihood, and may feel that this kind of representation is necessary. The 'friend' must also follow the protocols of the meeting. The rules may say that the 'friend' should not speak directly to the panel. The 'friend' is there to be consulted by the complainant or practitioner, to help them to hear clearly what is being said and advise them. The name of the 'friend' and the nature of his or her professional expertise must be communicated to the panel within a certain time before the hearings and circulated to all parties, since each has the right to make reasonable objection to the 'friend' of the other.

## SUBMISSIONS

Requests for all written submissions and names of those who are being brought to give supportive testimony need to be made to ensure that there is enough time to reproduce and circulate the papers to all parties so that they may be considered before the adjudication. The clerk or designated person will need to check with the complainant and practitioner what papers constitute their final submission. This is particularly important if the adjudication is a separate process following an investigation.

## THE PROTOCOLS OF THE ADJUDICATION MEETING

The purpose of the adjudication meeting is to clarify the evidence given to support the allegations of the complainant and to hear the response of the practitioner. The panel will need to have given some time to the submissions, both individually to study them and together to discuss all aspects of the matter.

The protocol needs to allow time for both the panel and the parties to have the opportunity to question one another and their witnesses, so that the meeting can discover as much as possible and also be seen to be fair to all concerned.

The panel may decide that they want to question Rose about how she feels she was identified in Ray's paper, how her partner and colleague recognized her or whether she first drew their attention to what was being said, and whether there was material revealed in the paper that is unquestionably hers and in Ray's possession alone. Then they might decide that they want to question Ray about what he said in the lecture, where he may have varied from his transcript, and how he deals with case material that involves the physical humiliation of individuals. They may decide to be particularly tough in their questioning in certain areas.

With Sue they may want to recheck dates, particularly those where therapy and the sexual relationship were concurrent. Then she might be asked about her conversations with Jane and the supportive statements that she brings. Jane might wish to appear in support of Sue. They might question Trevor about the charges raised by Sue and Jane and how he can defend himself. In some cases those who have sex with patients do not hide the facts but see their patients as willing partners.

The protocol for a single-stage process needs to allow for two or more opportunities to question each party. The parties will normally be in the same room and statements made by one can be checked for agreement with the other.

In a case where there has possibly been considerable abuse of professional power it may be particularly hard for the complainant to bring the complaint, and it may have required a considerable working out and resolution of the transference with the former therapist. For example if Sue meets Trevor again in the adjudication room it may not help the management of the process. If the complainant is going to be too distressed then the complaints committee needs to decide if the panel should see the parties separately. The adjudication itself might become a re-enactment of the original circumstances of the complaint. It is helpful for organizations to allow flexibility in their protocols. However, they need to realize that if the meetings are held separately they may be exposing themselves to claims of unfairness. In legal terms, it is not acceptable for evidence to be given which the practitioner is not party to.

The panel will need to take regular breaks in order to discuss the progress of the adjudication. At these times the parties are asked to leave the room and are escorted to separate waiting rooms. Someone who is outside the meeting needs to be available to be with each group so that they do not meet outside the room, even when seeking refreshment or going to the lavatory.

If the case of David and Barbara came to adjudication the interviewers would speak to them together and hear both accounts of the events and both points of view. Then they might take a break and decide that they want clear evidence of contract-making from Barbara and also to explore David's confusion about verbal contract-making and the kind of therapy he was entering.

Sue and Trevor's case is more challenging, since in the eyes of the law and therefore most likely in the eyes of a judge conducting a judicial review, the more serious the offence the more clear the evidence must be before sanction is applied. Thus those hearing Trevor's case need to be competent individuals capable of very clear thinking, whose decisions will be respected and who can be seen by the professional community at large to make sound and proper recommendations, because they are going to decide the professional future of their colleague. Thus their lines of questioning need to be clear; they need clear statements from Sue and her supporters, they need to question Trevor and clarify matters with him, and they must return again to both parties until they are persuaded that they are clear about the matters before them and can take a view. It may well be that someone in Trevor's position will not deny the charges but will spend his time introducing charm and confusions and niggling questions into the meeting, attempting gradually to undermine the position and integrity of the complainant. The adjudicators need to be on their guard because there will be other Trevors who will be interested to hear the outcome of the hearing.

In all hearings, investigations or adjudications it is very important that members of the panels or those working outside supporting the proceedings of the meeting do not answer any questions or express any opinions about the matter being heard or any opinion about the outcome. They are all either servants of or appointees of the complaints committee and of the governing council of the organization concerned, and are participating in a hearing on their behalf. An informal discussion at the end of a hearing when one party has left can give a complainant or practitioner a sense that he or she knows the decision and can predict the outcome. The considered opinions of the adjudicators belong in their report backed up by whatever evidence they have to support it. The opinions of those stage-managing the event are in fact gossip, since they are not party to the papers and information, in a matter where confidentiality is all-important.

## THE REPORT

The adjudicators need to consider whether Rose, David or Sue has made a convincing case or whether there is no case to answer. They need to write their report supported by the evidence and followed with clear decisions. Their report belongs to the complaints committee, who will accept or not accept it.

Let us say that Ray was found to have breached Rose's confidence by clearly using her material, and the adjudicators saw this as un-professional. However, they did not find any evidence of disrespectful behaviour to the patient in terms of having treated her material in a voyeuristic manner. They would write their report to this effect, stating the evidence which supports these opinions.

In the case of David and Barbara, they may have felt that David had no previous experience or knowledge of therapy and therefore he had entered psychotherapy not understanding the nature of the commit-ment. Having lost Barbara's pamphlet he became confused. In the view of the adjudicators the pamphlet may have been inadequate, and, though the letters of her qualifications were in it, it did not explain the nature of her training or her methods of working or experience. However, she might be considered a competent practitioner.

In Sue and Trevor's case it might go one of two ways. Trevor may have confessed and agreed that the evidence provided by Sue was accurate; this would allow for a very unequivocal report. On the other hand, he may have denied the charges utterly and the adjudicators may have no clear or decisive evidence: it is one person's word against another's. Even so they are going to need to take a view on the evidence that has been presented to them.

The report does not need to be long. It needs to give the factual evidence for and against each count or clause of the code of practice cited in the complaint, and then to give the opinion of the adjudicators.

## THE DELIBERATIONS OF THE COMPLAINTS COMMITTEE

The complaints committee will meet to receive the report of the adjudication panel and consider its findings. If it accepts the report then it will need to decide what sanctions are to be suggested to the governing council of the organization.

# Chapter 12

# Outcomes, sanctions and appeals

Each organization should have included in its procedures the possibility of using a range of sanctions. Professional bodies generally do not see sanctions as being punishment for the practitioner's past misconduct but as protection of future vulnerable clients. It is this that the committee will have in mind when deciding on appropriate sanctions.

Once a case has been investigated and adjudicated there should be clear outcomes from those processes. The complaints committee then needs to consider which sanction or sanctions are appropriate and make a recommendation to the managing body of the organization. In psychotherapy and counselling we are moving away from a secret world in which complaints were formerly managed out of the public eye. The organization concerned and the profession in general need to know that matters of this kind are being properly attended to so that the public may gain a sense that psychotherapy and counselling organizations are dealing with their own problems and keeping their own houses in order. Though the details of complaints may never be known, any sanctions imposed are increasingly being publicized.

The complaints committee will know from the report of its adjudicators whether the practitioners concerned have breached their codes of ethics and practice. It is its task to consider the panel's report and decide upon the use of sanctions.

The object of sanctions is usually educative unless the matter is one of gross professional misconduct. The committee needs to address itself to two particular questions: those of client safety and practitioner competence. Are clients, trainees or supervisees safe with this particular practitioner, and is the practitioner fundamentally competent? The outcome and sanctions should directly relate to their judgement about these two questions.

The committee also needs to know the view of the umbrella

organization on such matters, since these views must guide and may restrict the committee in its deliberation, for instance its views on professional misconduct and gross professional misconduct. Professional misconduct is a conscious or actual breach of the code of ethics and practice of the organization; gross professional misconduct involves exploitation, whether financial, sexual or emotional, of the client, trainee or supervisee concerned.

In the complaint against Trevor, if Sue's complaint is upheld and Trevor does not contest it, however sympathetic the complaints committee may feel towards Trevor because he has always been polite and charming to the committee, the umbrella organization would see Trevor's breach as gross professional misconduct. The appropriate sanction is therefore removal of Trevor's professional status and his removal from their register. The deliberate nature of his offence would make it hard for the organization to believe that education would be effective or rehabilitation possible.

There are clear parallels in the professions supplementary to medicine where the public wants matters of exploitation to be dealt with severely. These views would inform the complaints committee. If Trevor were given a lesser sanction, Sue might appeal to the umbrella organization and have the sanction reconsidered.

If termination of membership is proposed then the committee should advise as to whether it should be permanent or say for three years or five years: and whether the organization should at any point consider restoring the membership.

Breaches of the codes of ethics and practice are often far more difficult to decide about than clear-cut cases. Most members of complaints committees will have an idea of what they consider to be competent and incompetent and should also have a good sense of present thinking about these issues. If client safety is not at stake the committee will need to consider the practitioner's competence, and whether the practitioner concerned should be subject to a punitive sanction, or if he or she is capable of change through learning.

Sanctions might include loss of status within the organization, say no longer working as a trainer or supervisor or as a therapist to those in training. Committees may feel that they wish to impose such a sanction but should realize that it may be difficult to implement.

Teaching work can be removed from the practitioner. However, supervision work and therapeutic work are far more difficult to remove, because they both involve transferential relationships. Should the organization wish to remove supervisory responsibilities it may need to do so over a limited time frame, while the stopping of therapeutic work is so complex that it needs only to be considered if it is believed that the practitioner may be incompetent and cannot change. Another solution may be that no more work of this kind is allocated to a particular practitioner either for a period of time or ever again.

The complaints committee must form a view as to whether Ray's breaching of Rose's confidence had been a one-off event, a calculated risk he had taken because he believed her to be abroad, or whether it was symptomatic of breaches of confidence generally in his work. The crux of its decision will depend on whether it believes that he has understanding of the cause of complaint and its meaning in his work. If he does then the sanction could possibly be more limited. If not the committee may feel that it needs to be more severe. Since he is a senior member of his organization it may wish to curtail his practice in some way. It might suggest, for instance, that Ray can no longer be a training therapist or supervisor for the organization. Or the committee might feel that it was not appropriate for him to be supervising trainees, and decide to remove this status from him. It might also suggest that he enter a period of supervision himself, or further therapy.

However, there may be a clear sense that the practitioner can learn and the committee might therefore suggest a review, with a senior practitioner, of his practice in a particular area, or a review of his total practice with a suggestion of limitation, supervision of the whole or part of the practice, further consultation, therapy or training.

In the cases of mistakes and incompetence it is often most difficult to make the sanctions appropriate. Questions centred on the symbolic nature of the complaint may come into the committee's deliberations. For example does the complaint reflect a one-off happening or a far deeper and more complex difficulty? For instance if David's complaint against Barbara were upheld, it could be that it was felt that Barbara had in this one instance made an inadequate contract because of the particular circumstances at David's first session. However, the committee might believe that the report indicated that there could be considerable difficulties in Barbara's practice not only in contract-making but in other areas too. They might decide that the appropriate sanction would be that she should completely review her practice with a senior practitioner and then for the duration of the sanction that she work under weekly supervision.

Sanctions need to be clearly stated, as does their duration, either in terms of time or improvement. If consultation or supervisory reports are required by the complaints committee then this needs to be stated. These are the conditions of sanction compliance. If analysis or therapy is recommended, frequency and duration must again be clearly stated. If further training is the requirement, proof of training satisfactorily completed may also be required.

Failure to be clear when sanctioning practitioners has caused considerable difficulty in the past. Practitioners expelled from organizations have sought to join other groups or to re-join their own organization within two years. Practitioners who have been believed to be too sick or too old and have said that they were retired or retiring, have suddenly found a new lease of life when the complaints committee of their organization no longer had jurisdiction over them. Practitioners who have been asked to find supervisors to oversee their sanction compliance have used their friends, though these relationships were not declared at the time to the complaints committee. The supervisors have thus been collusive and little or nothing has been learnt. Further complaints have then been made to the organization. Those referred for therapy or for training have done the absolute minimum and paid what has seemed like lip-service to compliance.

For these reasons it is important that the complaints committee is absolutely clear about the nature of the sanctions, the intensity or frequency of the sanctions and what the expected outcome of the sanctions is expected to be. Lack of rigour in these matters often results in very frustrated complaints committees who feel that their concern and work is not valued. Once the sanctions have been agreed and imposed they should never be increased except as the result of an appeal.

The committee needs to make itself absolutely clear in reporting back to its council or management group. It is not conducive to the maintenance of confidentiality to have the guts of the case totally reviewed by the management group. The council or management group has vested the power of managing and dealing with complaints in their complaints committee and it needs to finish the job, however difficult it may find it. It is sometimes very helpful if, at this point, an outside group therapist or analyst can be approached to facilitate and overview the decision-making process. This helps the committee keep to the point of the discussion and not act in some untoward way, drawn by personal allegiances. It needs to take a view and then consider the appropriate sanctions with that in mind.

The complaints committee, through its chair, will need to make its recommendations known to the council or management group. Since matters of complaint often need to be reported in an appropriate way from the complaints committee to the management of the organization, it is usual for the chair of the organization to be aware that there is a complaint and of its progress. However neither the members of the council of management nor the chair should know the content unless they are either members of the complaints committee or have taken part in investigatory or adjudicatory procedures. Once the final report has been given it is usual that the council accepts it and informs the parties to the complaint of its decision and of any sanctions that it is imposing.

Barbara may in her turn feel that the sanctions imposed against her are far too severe and, since the matter was not handled according to the organization's procedures and took far too long, she will appeal. It might be that Ray was exonerated by the complaints committee because it felt that there was not enough evidence to support Rose's claim. Or Trevor may feel that the termination of his membership of his organization is unfair. All may consider appealing against the council's decision. If a case was closed at investigation the complainant may also wish to appeal against this decision.

Any individual who, having brought a complaint or been the subject of a complaint, believes that the decision which has been found is not just, needs to have the opportunity to appeal and may wish to do so. This is a matter of natural justice.

In counselling and psychotherapy the organization should consider what grounds of appeal they are prepared to consider and inform the practitioner of that decision. Grounds for appeal are normally of three kinds. First there are appeals against the findings of the committee, either where there is relevant new evidence; or where the finding itself is considered unsatisfactory; or where the sanction imposed is considered unsatisfactory. Second, there are appeals where the procedure has not been used or operated correctly, known as appeals against the process of a complaint. Finally, there are appeals against membership of the organization being terminated. Let us consider each in turn.

Rose appeals against the finding on the grounds that Ray's breach of confidentiality is a breach of common law and also that she can provide new evidence. Since the adjudication, two colleagues have been contacted and are willing to make statements. They had all thought that Rose had a watertight case and therefore did not previously feel willing to come forward and be seen by Ray's colleagues as trouble-makers in a small community.

Appeals against the procedure or the way that the complaint has been managed are usual when a complex procedure has been used. Barbara may complain that the organization did not follow its own procedures properly and that she wants the decision overturned. It may have been that in this particular organization one person investigated a complaint and three people adjudicated it, and the whole process took eight months. The procedures state that there should be two investigators and that the process should take only six months from beginning to end. There are therefore clear grounds for appeal.

Trevor is appealing against the finding and against the sanction. He is incensed at his treatment by an organization for which and with which he has worked for fifteen years. Since he was so honest with his colleagues he feels that they have treated him very badly. He also has decided that he will approach his lawyer and consider pursuing a case in the courts since the termination of his membership would be a restriction on his right to earn his livelihood by practising his profession.

Appeals need to be heard quickly. It may well be appropriate that the appeal is heard within the organization itself. The organization needs to concern itself with content as well as with procedure. Those who hear an appeal are usually the president or chair of an organization. The person who holds this position needs to have been separate from the complaint until this stage and know little or nothing of the content. He or she will hear the appeal with one or two other 'wise' people. It is increasingly seen as a matter of good practice for there to be an outside person, either a co-professional, or a person from another psychologically based profession or a profession supplementary to medicine, included as a member of the panel. Certainly the use of an independent outsider is being encouraged by the officials of government departments like the Department of Health, since it is seen as a part of making processes and procedures of organizations more transparent and accountable.

Appeals can be heard in person in some suitable fashion or they can be reviewed on paper. Whether the organization decides to hear it in person or not may depend on the severity of the complaint or sanction. So often the documents speak for themselves; but the organization may feel that those involved should be heard so that they may see that every effort has been made to be impartial. As has been said before, the matter of how complainant and complained against perceive that they have been dealt with will be of the greatest importance if the outcome of the complaint is to be felt to be satisfactory by all concerned.

Those who appeal against their membership being terminated, under the Articles of Association, because their organization believes that they have by their behaviour brought the profession into disrepute, should be mentioned here. Under these circumstances the member has the right of appeal against the decision. This kind of an appeal involves the member summoning all the evidence that he or she can in self-defence and attempting to overturn the decision of the complaints committee or the council of management of the organization which invoked the expulsion.

The papers for any appeal will include those which the appellant wishes to include, supported by a statement giving the reason for an appeal. Any findings or reports can be part of this process. The other party to the complaint needs to be informed that there has been an appeal and to be given a date by which they will be told of the outcome. The process of appeal is to the organization and does not involve the other party to the complaint. If the appeal is on grounds of procedure, the chair of the complaints committee will need to defend the committee's operation of the procedure.

The people who hear the appeal need to assure themselves that the matter has been dealt with properly. If the appeal is about procedure they will need to review all the papers together with the complaints procedure to assure themselves that the procedure was meticulously followed and all hearings were acceptable in terms of natural justice.

If the appeal is about content, then the person reviewing it will need to consider whether the evidence is that the breaches of the code of ethics and of practice happened or not. They will particularly need to look at each report and see if they agree with the findings of investigators and adjudicators. The person reviewing the appeal will also need to consider whether the complaints committee's conclusions, as a result of these reports, were sound.

If the appeal involves both procedure and content it might be wise for the person who is hearing the appeal to consider the two matters separately, since such a way of approaching things often sheds light on what may by now be a fairly confused situation with feelings running high on all sides.

It may be helpful, for both the appellant and the organization, if the person who is hearing the appeal makes notes which can form the basis of a report, either upholding or not upholding the decisions of the ethics committee. Each part of the procedure needs to be reviewed, likewise each count on which the complaint has been made needs to be examined.

The outcome of an appeal is usually considered to be final and it is for this reason that the organization needs to have managed the process fairly and well, otherwise the complainant might feel persuaded to pursue the matter in the courts or consider taking the matter to a judicial review, particularly if the outcome seriously affects his or her ability to earn a living.

Sometimes an appeal to the organization is not the end of the matter and the complainant decides to pursue the matter with the umbrella organizations such as the BAC and the UKCP who allow further appeal. They may ask one or two individuals to review the complaint further on grounds of substance or procedure and examine the whole process that has taken place within the member organization.

Other parties to a complaint may pursue the case further by writing letters and even making accusations against particular individuals or organizations. If the individual pursues the matter in this way and everyone concerned is fully persuaded that all the proper processes have been gone through, there is little anyone can do. If the complaint has been managed well and the outcome was fair and reasonable these letters need acknowledgement; but the organization may have to decide that the matter has to be stopped and make this clear to the individual concerned. Then the individual will have to consider whether he or she wishes to pursue it in another way, such as through the courts.

# Conclusions

The challenge to psychotherapy and counselling nowadays, and my intention in writing this book, is to acknowledge that times have changed and our professional affairs can no longer be dealt with in secret, as in the past they may have been. The world outside has a view of justice which involves transparency and openness. The government expects it, it supports the internal policing of professions and the establishment of registers hoping to avoid legislative intervention.

We, as practitioners, are responding to this with a growing understanding that complaints and grievances need to be dealt with in a rigorous and fair way. It may seem ironic to fellow practitioners that there is any need to underline the principles of justice and fairness, as I have done, because these are usually considered to be central guiding principles in our work. However, when a complaint is made defensiveness is a usual response.

Presently, one of the greatest challenges to the profession is whether it can manage itself without external regulation. An ingredient in that challenge is whether we can maintain standards effectively. Managing grievances and complaints appropriately helps to maintain standards. The test for psychotherapy and counselling will be whether the relatively small organizations that are the component parts of the umbrella organizations can manage these processes adequately themselves or whether, if they cannot, they can be trusting enough to commit themselves to the central management of complaints, as happens in the BPS.

The quality of each organization's codes and complaints procedures will be of the greatest significance, as will be their effective implementation. If the organizations can manage these processes effectively then the self-regulating professions of psychotherapy and counselling are likely to be regarded in legal processes as being on a par with those which are regulated by statute.

It is therefore important to remember that there is usually something in a complaint indicating some individual or organizational difficulty that needs to be taken seriously. Organizations are wise to attend to grievances and complaints, especially if they come up with any frequency. There is a need to understand what they mean to the individual or individuals concerned and whether there is a parallel process involving the organization as a whole.

What must always be borne in mind is the bravery involved in making a complaint. It is much easier to close down on a bad experience. Pathologizing the patient or colleague who has made a complaint is all too easy, and unfortunately it happens all too frequently. Instead of being perceived as a source of fear or panic, complaints could be taken as an opportunity for learning in its broadest sense.

I hope that this book will help to allay fears and assist in the potentially difficult management of grievances and complaints because it is essential that we all answer the need for public accountability and that our standards should be above reproach.

# Addresses

British Association for Counselling
1 Regent Place
Rugby CV21 2PJ
(Tel: 01788 550899  Fax: 01788 562189  e-mail: bac@bac.co.uk)
The BAC publishes the *Counselling and Psychotherapy Resources Directory*.

The British Confederation of Psychotherapists
37 Mapesbury Road
London NW2 4HJ
(Tel: 0181 830 5173  Fax: 0181 452 3684)
The BCP publishes the *Register of Psychotherapists*.

The British Psychological Society
St Andrews House
48 Princess Road East
Leicester LE1 7DR
(Tel: 0116 254 9568  Fax: 0116 247 0787  e-mail: mail@bps.org.uk)

Confederation of Scottish Counselling Agencies (COSCA)
c/o D. McFadzean
64 Murray Place
Stirling SK8 2BX
(Tel: 01786 475140)

Prevention of Professional Abuse Network (POPAN)
1 Wyvil Close
10 Wyvil Road
London SW8 2TG
(Tel: 0171 622 6334)
POPAN is an agency which supports and assists patients wishing to bring complaints against health care professionals.

United Kingdom Council for Psychotherapy
167–169 Great Portland Street
London W1N 5FB
(Tel: 0171 436 3002)
The UKCP publishes the *National Register of Psychotherapists*.

# Codes of Ethics and Practice and Ethical Guidelines

## THE BRITISH ASSOCIATION FOR COUNSELLING

The BAC Code of Ethics and Practice for Counsellors has evolved since it was first produced in 1979. Now in its fourth version, this code is a well tried document. The codes have been actively used as a way of promoting standards of good practice for counsellors; they have always been seen as educative.

The BAC also publishes Codes of Ethics and Practice for Supervisors and for Trainers which are based on the Code for Counsellors.

## CODE OF ETHICS AND PRACTICE FOR COUNSELLORS

### 1 Status of this Code

In response to the experience of members of BAC, this code is a revision of the (1992) 1993 code, amended by the Management Committee (May 1996).

### 2 Introduction

2.1 The purpose of this code is to establish and maintain standards for counsellors who are members of BAC, and to inform and protect people who seek or use their services.

2.2 All members of this Association are required to abide by the current codes appropriate to them. Implicit in these codes is a common frame of reference within which members manage their responsibilities to clients, colleagues, members of BAC and the wider community. No code can resolve all issues relating to ethics and practice. In this code we aim to provide a framework for addressing ethical issues and encouraging best possible levels of practice. Members must determine which parts apply to particular settings, taking account of any conflicting responsibilities.

2.3 The Association has a Complaints Procedure which can lead to the expulsion of members for breaches of its Codes of Ethics and Practice.

# 3 The nature of counselling

3.1 The overall aim of counselling is to provide an opportunity for the client to work towards living in a way he or she experiences as more satisfying and resourceful. The term 'counselling' includes work with individuals, pairs or groups of people often, but not always, referred to as 'clients'. The objectives of particular counselling relationships will vary according to the client's needs. Counselling may be concerned with developmental issues, addressing and resolving specific problems, making decisions, coping with crisis, developing personal insight and knowledge, working through feelings of inner conflict or improving relationships with others. The counsellor's role is to facilitate the client's work in ways which respect the client's values, personal resources and capacity for choice within his or her cultural context.

3.2 Counselling involves a deliberately undertaken contract with clearly agreed boundaries and commitment to privacy and confidentiality. It requires explicit and informed agreement. The use of counselling skills in other contexts, paid or voluntary, is subject to the Code of Ethics and Practice for Counselling Skills.

3.3 There is no generally accepted distinction between counselling and psychotherapy. There are well founded traditions which use the terms interchangeably and others which distinguish between them. Regardless of the theoretical approaches preferred by individual counsellors, there are ethical issues which are common to all counselling situations.

# 4 Equal Opportunities Policy Statement

'The British Association for Counselling' (BAC) is committed to promoting Equality of Opportunity of access and participation for all its members in all of its structures and their workings. BAC has due regard for those groups of people with identifiable characteristics which can lead to visible and invisible barriers thus inhibiting their joining and full participation in BAC. Barriers can include age, colour, creed, culture, disability, education, 'ethnicity', gender, information, knowledge, mobility, money, nationality, race, religion, sexual orientation, social class and status.

The work of BAC aims to reflect this commitment in all areas including services to members, employer responsibilities, the recruitment of and working with volunteers, setting, assessing, monitoring and evaluating standards and the implementation of the complaints procedures. This is particularly important as BAC is the 'Voice of Counselling' in the wider world.

BAC will promote and encourage commitment to Equality of Opportunity by its members.

## 5 The structure of this Code

This code has been divided into two parts. The Code of Ethics outlines the fundamental values of counselling and a number of general principles arising from these. The Code of Practice applies these principles to the counselling situation.

## A CODE OF ETHICS

### Values

Counsellors' basic values are integrity, impartiality and respect.

### A.1 Responsibility

All reasonable steps should be taken to ensure the client's safety during counselling sessions. Counselling is a non-exploitative activity. Counsellors must take the same degree of care to work ethically whatever the setting or the financial basis of the counselling contract.

### A.2 Anti-discriminatory practice

Counsellors must consider and address their own prejudices and stereotyping and ensure that an anti-discriminatory approach is integral to their counselling practice.

### A.3 Confidentiality

Counsellors offer the highest possible levels of confidentiality in order to respect the client's privacy and create the trust necessary for counselling.

## A.4 Contracts

The terms and conditions on which counselling is offered shall be made clear to clients before counselling begins. Subsequent revision of these terms should be agreed in advance of any changes.

## A.5 Boundaries

Counsellors must establish and maintain appropriate boundaries around the counselling relationship. Counsellors must take into account the effects of any overlapping or pre-existing relationships.

## A.6 Competence

Counsellors shall take all reasonable steps to monitor and develop their own competence and to work within the limits of that competence. Counsellors must have appropriate, regular and ongoing counselling supervision.

## B CODE OF PRACTICE

### Introduction

This code applies these values and ethical principles outlined above to more specific situations which may arise in the practice of counselling. The sections and clauses are arranged in the order of the ethics section and under the same headings. **No clause or section should be read in isolation from the rest of the Code**.

### B.1 Issues of responsibility

B.1.1 The counsellor–client relationship is the foremost ethical concern. However, counselling does not exist in social isolation. Counsellors may need to consider other sources of ethical responsibility. The headings in this section are intended to draw attention to some of these.

B.1.2 Counsellors take responsibility for clinical/therapeutic decisions in their work with clients.

*B.1.3    Responsibility to the client*

Client safety

B.1.3.1 Counsellors must take all reasonable steps to ensure that the client suffers neither physical nor psychological harm during counselling sessions.

B.1.3.2 Counsellors must not exploit their clients financially, sexually, emotionally, or in any other way. Suggesting or engaging in sexual activity with a client is unethical.

B.1.3.3 Counsellors must provide privacy for counselling sessions. The sessions should not be overheard, recorded or observed by anyone other than the counsellor without informed consent from the client. Normally any recording would be discussed as part of the contract. Care must be taken that sessions are not interrupted.

Client self-determination

B.1.3.4 In counselling the balance of power is unequal and counsellors must take care not to abuse their power.

B.1.3.5 Counsellors do not normally act on behalf of their clients. If they do, it will be only at the express request of the client, or else in exceptional circumstances.

B.1.3.6 Counsellors do not normally give advice.

B.1.3.7 Counsellors have a responsibility to establish with clients at the outset of counselling the existence of any other therapeutic or helping relationships in which the client is involved and to consider whether counselling is appropriate. Counsellors should gain the client's permission before conferring in any way with other professional workers.

Breaks and endings

B.1.3.8 Counsellors work with clients to reach a recognised ending when clients have received the help they sought or when it is apparent that counselling is no longer helping or when clients wish to end.

B.1.3.9 External circumstances may lead to endings for other reasons which are not therapeutic. Counsellors must make arrangements for care to be taken of the immediate needs of clients in the event of any sudden and unforeseen endings by the counsellor or breaks to the counselling relationship.

B.1.3.10 Counsellors should take care to prepare their clients appropriately for any planned breaks from counselling. They should take any necessary steps to ensure the well-being of their clients during such breaks.

## B.1.4    Responsibility to other counsellors

B.1.4.1    Counsellors must not conduct themselves in their counselling-related activities in ways which undermine public confidence either in their role as a counsellor or in the work of other counsellors.

B.1.4.2    A counsellor who suspects misconduct by another counsellor which cannot be resolved or remedied after discussion with the counsellor concerned, should implement the Complaints Procedure, doing so without breaches of confidentiality other than those necessary for investigating the complaint.

## B.1.5    Responsibility to colleagues and others

B.1.5.1    Counsellors are accountable for their services to colleagues, employers and funding bodies as appropriate. At the same time they must respect the privacy, needs and autonomy of the client as well as the contract of confidentiality agreed with the client.

B.1.5.2    No-one should be led to believe that a service is being offered by the counsellor which is not in fact being offered, as this may deprive the client of the offer of such a service from elsewhere.

B.1.5.3    Counsellors must play their part in exploring and resolving conflicts of interest between themselves and their employers or agencies, especially where this has implications for the client.

## B.1.6    Responsibility to the wider community

Law

B.1.6.1    Counsellors must take all reasonable steps to be aware of current law as it applies to their counselling practice. (See BAC Information Guide 1 'Counselling, Confidentiality and the Law'.)

Research

B.1.6.2    Counsellors must conduct any research in accordance with BAC guidelines (see BAC Information Guide 4 'Ethical Guidelines for Monitoring, Evaluation and Research in Counselling').

Resolving conflicts between ethical priorities

B.1.6.3    Counsellors may find themselves caught between conflicting ethical principles, which could involve issues of public interest. In these circumstances, they are urged to consider the particular situation in which they find themselves and to discuss the situation with their counselling supervisor and/or other experienced counsellors. Even after conscientious consideration of the salient issues, some ethical dilemmas cannot be resolved easily or wholly satisfactorily.

## B.2    Anti-discriminatory practice

Client respect

B.2.1    Counsellors work with clients in ways that affirm both the common humanity and the uniqueness of each individual. They must be sensitive to the cultural context and world view of the client, for instance whether the individual, family or the community is taken as central.

Client autonomy

B.2.2    Counsellors are responsible for working in ways which respect and promote the client's ability to make decisions in the light of his/her own beliefs, values and context.

Counsellor awareness

B.2.3    Counsellors are responsible for ensuring that any problems with mutual comprehension due to language, cultural differences or for any other reason are addressed at an early stage. The use of an interpreter needs to be carefully considered at the outset of counselling.

B.2.4    Counsellors have a responsibility to consider and address their own prejudices and stereotyping attitudes and behaviour and particularly to consider ways in which these may be affecting the counselling relationship and influencing their responses.

## B.3    Confidentiality

B.3.1    Confidentiality is a means of providing the client with safety and privacy and thus protects client autonomy. For this reason any limitation on the degree of confidentiality is likely to diminish the effectiveness of counselling.

B.3.2    The counselling contract will include an agreement about the level and limits of confidentiality offered. This agreement can be reviewed and changed by negotiation between counsellor and client. Agreements about confidentiality continue after the client's death unless there are overriding legal or ethical considerations.

## B.3.3    Settings

B.3.3.1 Counsellors must ensure that they have taken all reasonable steps to inform the client of any limitations to confidentiality that arise within the setting of the counselling work, e.g. updating doctors in primary care, team case discussion in agencies. These are made explicit through clear contracting.

B.3.3.2 Many settings place additional specific limitations on confidentiality. Counsellors considering working in these settings must think about the impact of such limitations on their practice and decide whether or not to work in such settings.

## B.3.4    Exceptional circumstances

B.3.4.1 Exceptional circumstances may arise which give the counsellor good grounds for believing that serious harm may occur to the client or to other people. In such circumstances the client's consent to a change in the agreement about confidentiality should be sought whenever possible unless there are also good grounds for believing the client is no longer willing or able to take responsibility for his/her actions. Normally, the decision to break confidentiality should be discussed with the client and should be made only after consultation with the counselling supervisor or if he/she is not available, an experienced counsellor.

B.3.4.2 Any disclosure of confidential information should be restricted to relevant information, conveyed only to appropriate people and for appropriate reasons likely to alleviate the exceptional circumstances. The ethical considerations include achieving a balance between acting in the best interests of the client and the counsellor's responsibilities to the wider community.

B.3.4.3 Counsellors hold different views about the grounds for breaking confidentiality, such as potential self-harm, suicide, and harm to others. Counsellors must consider their own views, as they will affect their practice and communicate them to clients and significant others, e.g. supervisor, agency.

### B.3.5 Management of confidentiality

B.3.5.1 Counsellors should ensure that records of the client's identity are kept separately from any case notes.

B.3.5.2 Arrangements must be made for the safe disposal of client records, especially in the event of the counsellor's incapacity or death.

B.3.5.3 Care must be taken to ensure that personally identifiable information is not transmitted through overlapping networks of confidential relationships.

B.3.5.4 When case material is used for case studies, reports or publications the client's informed consent must be obtained wherever possible and their identity must be effectively disguised.

B.3.5.5 Any discussion about their counselling work between the counsellor and others should be purposeful and not trivialising.

B.3.5.6 Counsellors must pay particular attention to protecting the identity of clients. This includes discussion of cases in counselling supervision.

## B.4 Contracts

### B.4.1 Advertising and public statements

B.4.1.1 Membership of BAC is not a qualification and it must not be used as if it were. In press advertisements and telephone directories, on business cards, letterheads, brass plates and plaques, etc. counsellors should limit the information to name, relevant qualifications, address, telephone number, hours available, a listing of the services offered and fees charged. They should not mention membership of BAC.

B.4.1.2 In oral statements, letters and pre-counselling leaflets to the public and potential clients, BAC membership may not be mentioned without a statement that it means that the individual, and where appropriate the organisation, abides by the Codes of Ethics and Practice and is subject to the Complaints Procedure of the British Association for Counselling. Copies of these Codes and the Complaints Procedure are available from BAC.

B.4.1.3 Counsellors who are accredited and/or registered are encouraged to mention this.

B.4.1.4 All advertising and public statements should be accurate in every particular.

B.4.1.5 Counsellors should not display an affiliation with an organisation in a manner which falsely implies sponsorship or validation by that organisation.

## B.4.2    Pre-counselling information

B.4.2.1   Any publicity material and all written and oral information should reflect accurately the nature of the service on offer, and the relevant counselling training, qualifications and experience of the counsellor.

B.4.2.2   Counsellors should take all reasonable steps to honour undertakings made in their pre-counselling information.

## B.4.3    Contracting with clients

B.4.3.1   Counsellors are responsible for reaching agreement with their clients about the terms on which counselling is being offered, including availability, the degree of confidentiality offered, arrangements for the payment of any fees, cancelled appointments and other significant matters. The communication of essential terms and any negotiations should be concluded by having reached a clear agreement before the client incurs any commitment or liability of any kind.

B.4.3.2   The counsellor has a responsibility to ensure that the client is given a free choice whether or not to participate in counselling. Reasonable steps should be taken in the course of the counselling relationship to ensure that the client is given an opportunity to review the counselling.

B.4.3.3   Counsellors must avoid conflicts of interest wherever possible. Any conflicts of interest that do occur must be discussed in counselling supervision and where appropriate with the client.

B.4.3.4   Records of appointments should be kept and clients should be made aware of this. If records of counselling sessions are kept, clients should also be made aware of this. At the client's request information should be given about access to these records, their availability to other people, and the degree of security with which they are kept.

B.4.3.5   Counsellors must be aware that computer-based records are subject to statutory regulations. It is the counsellor's responsibility to be aware of any changes the government may introduce in the regulations concerning the client's right of access to his/her records.

B.4.3.6   Counsellors are responsible for addressing any client dissatisfaction with the counselling.

## B.5    Boundaries

With clients

B.5.1    Counsellors are responsible for setting and monitoring boundaries throughout the counselling sessions and will make explicit to clients that counselling is a formal and contracted relationship and nothing else.

B.5.2    The counselling relationship must not be concurrent with a supervisory or training relationship.

With former clients

B.5.3    Counsellors remain accountable for relationships with former clients and must exercise caution over entering into friendships, business relationships, sexual relationships, training, supervising and other relationships. Any changes in relationship must be discussed in counselling supervision. The decision about any change(s) in relationship with former clients should take into account whether the issues and power dynamics present during the counselling relationship have been resolved.

B.5.4    Counsellors who belong to organisations which prohibit sexual activity with all former clients are bound by that commitment.

## B.6    Competence

### B.6.1    Counsellor competence

B.6.1.1    Counsellors must have achieved a level of competence before commencing counselling and must maintain continuing professional development as well as regular and ongoing supervision.

B.6.1.2    Counsellors must actively monitor their own competence through counselling supervision and be willing to consider any views expressed by their clients and by other counsellors.

B.6.1.3    Counsellors will monitor their functioning and will not counsel when their functioning is impaired by alcohol or drugs. In situations of personal or emotional difficulty, or illness, counsellors will monitor the point at which they are no longer competent to practise and take action accordingly.

B.6.1.4    Competence includes being able to recognise when it is appropriate to refer a client elsewhere.

B.6.1.5    Counsellors are responsible for ensuring that their relationships with clients are not unduly influenced by their own emotional needs.

B.6.1.6  Counsellors must consider the need for professional indemnity insurance and when appropriate take out and maintain adequate cover.

B.6.1.7  When uncertain as to whether a particular situation or course of action may be in violation of the Code of Ethics and Practice, counsellors must consult with their counselling supervisor and/or other experienced practitioners.

## B.6.2  Counsellor safety

B.6.2.1  Counsellors should take all reasonable steps to ensure their own physical safety.

## B.6.3  Counselling supervision

B.6.3.1  Counselling supervision refers to a formal arrangement which enables counsellors to discuss their counselling regularly with one or more people who are normally experienced as counselling practitioners and have an understanding of counselling supervision. Its purpose is to ensure the efficacy of the counsellor–client relationship. It is a confidential relationship.

B.6.3.2  The counselling supervisor role should wherever possible be independent of the line manager role. However, where a counselling supervisor is also line manager, the counsellor must have additional regular access to independent counselling supervision.

B.6.3.3  Counselling supervision must be regular, consistent and appropriate to the counselling. The volume should reflect the volume of counselling work undertaken and the experience of the counsellor.

## B.6.4  Awareness of other Codes

Counsellors must take account of the following Codes and Procedures adopted by the Annual General Meetings of the British Association for Counselling:

*Code of Ethics & Practice for Counselling Skills (1988)* applies to members who would not regard themselves as counsellors, but who use counselling skills to support other roles.

*Code of Ethics & Practice for Supervisors of Counsellors (1996)* applies to members offering supervision to counsellors and also helps counsellors seeking supervision.

*Code of Ethics & Practice for Trainers (1997)* applies to members offering training to counsellors and also helps members of the public seeking counselling training.

*Complaints Procedure (1994)* applies to members of BAC in the event of complaints about breaches of the Codes of Ethics & Practice.

Copies and other guidelines and information sheets relevant to maintaining ethical standards of practice can be obtained from the BAC office, 1 Regent Place, Rugby CV21 2PJ.

## THE BRITISH CONFEDERATION OF PSYCHOTHERAPISTS: PSYCHOANALYSTS, ANALYTICAL PSYCHOLOGISTS, PSYCHOANALYTIC PSYCHOTHERAPISTS AND CHILD PSYCHOTHERAPISTS

The BCP's present statement is a document which accepts that its constituent members have codes of ethics and practice which will have been monitored by the BCP. It is currently being revised. The constituent member organizations (institutions) of the BCP have complete autonomy within the limitations set out in the standards stated below.

## PART I STANDARDS FOR CODES OF ETHICS OF MEMBER ORGANISATIONS REQUIRED BY THE BCP CONSTITUTION AND GUIDELINES FOR MEMBERSHIP

### Part I A    Obligations under the BCP Constitution

Article 6 of the Constitution of the BCP requires that:

*6.1    In order to hold membership of the BCP, each organisation must have an appropriate Code of Ethics which must include at least the following features:*

i    a clear statement of the procedure to be followed in the event of a formal complaint of neglect or malpractice in connection with a member of that organisation, and

ii    a description of the disciplinary procedures which may be used, and which must allow as a sanction the possibility that a practitioner can be struck off the register and debarred from membership of the organisation.

## 6.2   *Professional Indemnity Insurance*

Each organisation must require, as a condition of membership, that all its members are covered by professional indemnity insurance.
Article 6 sets out further administrative conditions which affect member organisations.

## 6.3   *Removal from membership of the BCP*

i   The withdrawal from membership of the BCP by an organisation, or the withdrawal of its membership as a result of a decision of the Council of the Institutions of the BCP, will automatically lead to the withdrawal from the BCP Register of its list of members. (Article 16 of the BCP Constitution entitled 'Withdrawal of Membership', sets out the reasons and the procedure governing the withdrawal of membership.)

ii   The withdrawal by a member institution of the name of one of its members from its own Register will be followed automatically by the removal of the member's name from that institutions list on the register of the BCP.

## 6.4   *Obligations of Full and Affiliate Members*

i   As a condition of membership of the BCP, every organisation must ensure that an up-to-date copy of its Code of Ethics is lodged with the Registrar of the BCP.

ii   The Registrar of the BCP must be informed immediately of any further elaboration or alteration to an organisation's Code of Ethics.

iii   Should a member organisation remove a person from its own membership Register, it undertakes to inform any other member organisation of the BCP on whose Register the person is listed.

The document entitled 'Guidelines for Membership and Administrative Procedures' clarifies further the BCP policy and procedures concerning the Codes of Ethics of member institutions.

## Part 1 B Obligations under the Guidelines for Membership of the BCP

Part 7 of the document containing 'The Guidelines for Membership of the BCP' sets out the following expectations of member institutions:

7.1 The minimal requirement for an organisation's Code of Ethics is set out under Article 6 of the Constitution of the BCP.

7.2 The BCP shall not act as a body to which appeals can be taken: neither from a member organisation concerned about the professional conduct of any of its members, nor from psychoanalytic psychotherapists on the BCP's Register who may be in conflict with their institutions.

7.3 Enquiries about the codes of practice of member organisations, or complaints made to the BCP concerning the actions of any member organisation or psychoanalytic psychotherapists on the BCP Register must be referred to the relevant member institution for that institution to make an appropriate response.

7.4 As required under Article 6 of the Constitution, each institution must lodge with the Registrar of the BCP an up-to-date copy of its Code of Ethics, or an equivalent statement, outlining the disciplinary framework within which its members work.

7.5 Member organisations must inform the Registrar promptly, in writing, of any change in their Code of Ethics.

7.6 If, in the view of the Registration Committee of the BCP, changes to a member institution's Code of Ethics causes the Committee to judge that that institution may be in breach of the standards required for membership of the BCP, it will report the matter to the BCP Executive through the Chairman of the Executive Committee.

7.7 The Executive Committee of the BCP shall have the authority to conduct further enquiries. Once satisfied that the institution concerned is in breach of the requirements for Codes of Ethics set out in the BCP Constitution, the Chairman will report the matter to the Council of the BCP.

7.8 It will be for the Council to make a final judgement as to whether or not the institution is in breach of its obligations under the Constitution.

7.9 Should the BCP Council decide that an institution no longer fulfils its obligations under the Constitution in its provision of an appropriate Code of Ethics, it may decide to institute proceedings leading to the withdrawal of an organisation's membership of the BCP and the removal of the names of its members from the Register of the BCP.

# THE BRITISH PSYCHOLOGICAL SOCIETY

The BPS gives a clear statement to its members about Ethics and Practice; again this is a document tested through use and time.

# DIVISION OF COUNSELLING PSYCHOLOGY

# GUIDELINES FOR THE PROFESSIONAL PRACTICE OF COUNSELLING PSYCHOLOGY

## Introduction

Counselling Pyschology was first recognised within the British Psychological Society in 1982 when the Counselling Psychology Section was established. The rapid growth in membership, reflecting the escalating interest in the subject both nationally and inter-nationally, led to the Section becoming a Special Group in 1989 and finally a Division in 1994.

In formulating the Guidelines for Professional Practice in Counselling Psychology, set out below, the emphasis has been on setting out standards for exemplary practice. **They are to be taken as supplementary to the Society's *Code of Conduct, Ethical Principles and Guidelines*** which sets a bottom line below which behaviour should not fall. Breaches of the Code are identified as bad practice subject to disciplinary procedures.

The Guidelines, in contrast, seek to identify and recommend good practice. They are, therefore, expressed in terms of what counselling psychologists are expected to do in terms of the pursuit of best practice. Whilst the implementation of the Guidelines is left to the judgement of individual practitioners and subject to their particular circumstances, actions and practices which are contrary to the recommendations warrant serious and careful consideration in consultation with supervisors. The real needs of the situation, rather than expediency, personal convenience, prejudice or profit, should be the determining factors in all cases.

These Guidelines are the result of consulting many practitioners, the Guidelines of other Divisions, particularly those of the Division of Clinical Psychology and the Codes of Ethics and Practice of the British Association for Counselling. They constitute a working document that will be revised and up-dated every three years in the light of experience and changes both within the discipline and in the context of practice.

*Counselling psychology: a definition*

Historically, counselling psychology has developed as a branch of professional psychological practice strongly influenced by humanistic clinical practice and research as well as the psychodynamic and cognitive-behavioural psychotherapeutic traditions. Its relationship with mainstream academic psychology has not always been easy because counselling psychology has drawn upon and developed models of practice and enquiry which have often been at odds with the dominant conceptions of scientific psychology. Fruitful relationships have also been established with other counselling and psychotherapeutic practices which have evolved outside the framework of academic psychology.

Counselling psychology acknowledges these valued and continuing relationships whilst affirming its connections with mainstream professional psychological practice. It continues to develop models of practice and research which marry the scientific demand for rigorous empirical enquiry with a firm value base grounded in the primacy of the counselling/psychotherapeutic relationship. These models seek:

1  to engage with subjectivity and inter-subjectivity, values and feelings;
2  to know empathically and respect first-person accounts as valid in their own terms; to elucidate, interpret and negotiate between perceptions and world views but not to assume the automatic superiority of any one way of experiencing, feeling, valuing and knowing;
3  to be practice led, with a research base grounded in professional practice values as well as professional artistry;
4  to recognise social contexts and discrimination and to work always in ways which empower rather than control and towards high standards of anti-discriminatory practice appropriate to the pluralistic nature of society today.

*Structure and applicability of the guidelines*

The Guidelines for Professional Practice in Counselling Psychology are set out as follows:

The practitioner's responsibilities and obligations:

1  to self and client
2  to self and colleagues

In the context of these guidelines '**practitioner**' means all those members of the Division of Counselling Psychology who are practising counselling psychology whether accredited (Chartered) or in training.

# 1 PRACTITIONER'S OBLIGATIONS AND RESPONSIBILITIES TO SELF AND CLIENT

## 1.1 Competence

1.1.1 Following the Society's Code Section 2, practitioners will offer their best practice whilst recognising and not practising beyond their limitations in current training and ability. They continue throughout their careers to maintain and advance their knowledge and skills by undertaking and recording continuing professional development such as keeping abreast of the literature, broadening their experience, consulting with colleagues, attending workshops, courses and conferences, and regularly reviewing their own needs and performance. The supervision/consultancy relationship (see Section 2.1) is a key element in this process.

1.1.2 Accredited (Chartered) practitioners ensure that they are in possession of a current practising certificate irrespective of the amount or context of their practice.

## 1.2 Fitness to practise

1.2.1 Practitioners will continually monitor and maintain an effective level of personal functioning, i.e. should the practitioner feel unable to work effectively, help and advice will be sought from the supervisor/professional consultant. If necessary, the practitioner will withdraw for whatever time period is appropriate.

1.2.2 Practitioners will ensure that they hold adequate, professional indemnity and maintain their personal safety.

## 1.3 Respect for clients' autonomy

1.3.1 The practitioner will always seek to promote clients' control over their lives and their ability to make appropriate decisions, being mindful throughout of the power dynamics of the professional/client relationship.

1.3.2 Practitioners will respect the diversity of beliefs and values and will continually review their practice with due regard for changing societal norms.

1.3.3 In view of the personal and often intense nature of the therapeutic relationship practitioners will take particular care to avoid exploiting their clients financially, sexually, emotionally or in any other way.

Special regard will be paid to the Society's statement (in the Code) on Sexual Harassment and Dual Relationships. With respect to the latter, therapeutic relationships expressly preclude sexual relationships and all boundary issues will be carefully considered. Any concerns will be discussed with the supervisor/consultant and it is the practitioner's responsibility to define and maintain clear and appropriate boundaries.

1.3.4 The practitioner will normally work with approaches and procedures that can be made understandable to the client and to which clients can be asked to give their informed consent.

### 1.4  Contracting

1.4.1 Practitioners are responsible for making clear and explicit contracts.

1.4.2 Practitioners will inform clients of any financial liability before it is incurred.

1.4.3 Practitioners will inform clients of issues of confidentiality, including those pertaining to record keeping and supervision/consultancy, during the contracting process.

1.4.4 All contracts are subject to regular review.

### 1.5  Confidentiality

1.5.1 Rigorous respect for issues of confidentiality is fundamental to the successful practice of counselling psychology. The practitioner will clarify and explain the nature and extent of confidentiality from the start. Circumstances in which confidentiality may be breached will be identified.

1.5.2 Client records will be held securely at all times and the nature of records and clients' rights of access made clear. Practitioners will make provision for appropriate access to records and the informing of clients in the event of their own death or incapacity.

1.5.3 Agreements about confidentiality are expected to continue after a client's death unless legal and/or ethical considerations demand otherwise.

### 1.6 Confidentiality in the legal process

It is a fundamental responsibility of the practitioner to be aware of the specific legal implications of their work, including the general legal requirements concerning giving and withholding information, and to seek professional support and guidance as necessary.

The practitioner will ensure he or she has established channels for discussing legal issues with appropriately qualified people, in advance of the specific need.

## 2 PRACTITIONER'S RESPONSIBILITIES AND OBLIGATIONS TO SELF AND COLLEAGUES

### 2.1 Supervision and consultative support

2.1.1 Supervision/consultative support is a contractually negotiated relationship between practitioners with the purpose of supporting, evaluating and developing professional practice.

2.1.2 There is an ethical requirement for every practitioner to have regular supervision or consultative support from a suitably qualified co-professional.

2.1.3 The supervisory contract will be clearly defined, confidential, proportional to the volume of work and appropriate to the experience of the supervisee. The expectation for individual supervision is of 1.5 hours per month for a minimal case load, increasing proportionally with the case load.

2.1.4 It is very important that the supervisory relationship is clearly distinguished from any line-management responsibilities.

2.1.5 The relationship between the supervisor and supervisee will be characterised by mutual respect for competence and differing values, non-exploitation and good modelling.

2.1.6 The supervisor's role and responsibilities to the supervisee will be clearly negotiated and defined, particularly in respect of monitoring, maintaining and extending levels of effectiveness.

2.1.7 The supervisee's rights and responsibilities to the supervisor will be similarly negotiated and defined.

2.1.8 Whenever conflicts of interest, questions of ethical priority or legal issues arise supervisees will consult with supervisors.

2.1.9 The responsibility of both supervisor and supervisee to the client is paramount. However, responsibilities to others, for example, managers and colleagues, will also be carefully considered.

## 2.2 The practitioner as trainer

2.2.1 The trainer is responsible for the maintenance of adequate standards in the application of psychological principles and ethics, especially in promoting the welfare and rights of clients and in preserving the confidentiality of their case material.

2.2.2 The trainer is responsible for taking steps to ensure appropriate levels of training for trainees.

2.2.3 Levels of authority and legal responsibility will be negotiated by the trainer and complaints and disciplinary procedures made available to trainees.

2.2.4 The trainer will take steps to make clear, to appropriate others, the limitations of training programmes in relation to subsequent practice.

## 2.3 Boundaries and dual relationships in supervision and training

As in client/practitioner relationships, the personal and often intense nature of supervision and training relationships in counselling/ psychotherapy require practitioners to be especially sensitive to boundary issues and particularly careful in the area of dual relationships. Sexual relationships are precluded. Trainers and supervisors should avoid therapeutic contracts with trainees and supervisees. It is the responsibility of the practitioner to establish and maintain appropriate boundaries and to make complaints procedures available to trainees and supervisees.

## 2.4 The practitioner as researcher

2.4.1 It is expected that there will be congruence between the model of research chosen and the values of counselling psychology. Research will be designed and conducted in the spirit of the collaborative ways of working emphasised in counselling psychology. This will normally exclude such procedures as withholding of information, deception of clients, the manipulation of levels of stress and encroachment on personal privacy.

2.4.2 The individual's right to full information about the nature and value of research will be respected and clients must be able to give free, informed consent and to withdraw or withhold data without prejudice to their care.

2.4.3 Practitioners have an obligation to make the results of their research available to other professionals whilst respecting confidentiality.

## Conclusion

It is important to reiterate that the Guidelines as set out above are written in terms of general principles and it is the individual practitioner's responsibility to interpret them in terms of personal best practice in their particular circumstances. They are to be considered as part of the evolutionary process which constitutes the continuing professional development of the Division. As such constructive comments are warmly welcomed. **These should be directed to the Standing Committee for Professional Affairs via the Division Committee, Division of Counselling Psychology**.

# THE UNITED KINGDOM COUNCIL FOR PSYCHOTHERAPY

The UKCP, like the BCP, is an organization of organizations. They have developed guidelines which set standards for psychotherapy. They also give very clear guidance to their member organizations about what they expect from a code.

## ETHICAL REQUIREMENTS

### 1 Introduction

1.1 The purpose of a Code of Ethics is to define general principles and to establish standards of professional conduct for psychotherapists in their work and to inform and protect those members of the public who seek their services. Each organisation will include and elaborate upon the following principles in its Code of Ethics.

1.2 All psychotherapists are expected to approach their work with the aim of alleviating suffering and promoting the well-being of their clients.

Psychotherapists should endeavour to use their abilities and skills to their client's best advantage without prejudice and with due recognition of the value and dignity of every human being.

1.3 **All psychotherapists on the UKCP Register are required to adhere to the Codes of Ethics and Practice of their own organisations which will be consistent with the following statements and which will have been approved by the appropriate UKCP Section**.

## 2 Codes of Ethics

Each Member Organisation of UKCP must have published a Code of Ethics approved by the appropriate UKCP Section and appropriate for the practitioners of that particular organisation and their clients. The Code of Ethics will include and elaborate upon the following ten points to which attention is drawn here. All psychotherapists on the UKCP Register are required to adhere to the Codes of Ethics of their own organisations.

2.1 *Qualifications* – Psychotherapists are required to disclose their qualifications when requested and not claim, or imply, qualifications that they do not have.

2.2 *Terms, conditions and methods of practice* – Psychotherapists are required to disclose on request their terms, conditions and, where appropriate, methods of practice at the outset of psychotherapy.

2.3 *Confidentiality* – Psychotherapists are required to preserve confidentiality and to disclose, if requested, the limits of confidentiality and circumstances under which it might be broken to specific third parties.

2.4 *Professional relationship* – Psychotherapists should consider the client's best interest when making appropriate contact with the client's GP, relevant psychiatric services, or other relevant professionals with the client's knowledge. Psychotherapists should be aware of their own limitations.

2.5 *Relationship with clients* – Psychotherapists are required to maintain appropriate boundaries with their clients. They must take care to not exploit their clients, current or past, in any way, financially, sexually or emotionally.

2.6 *Research* – Psychotherapists are required to clarify with clients the nature, purpose and conditions of any research in which the clients are to be involved and to ensure that informed and verifiable consent is given before commencement.

2.7 *Publication* – Psychotherapists are required to safeguard the welfare and anonymity of clients when any form of publication of clinical material is considered and to obtain their consent whenever possible.

2.8 *Practitioner competence* – Psychotherapists are required to maintain their ability to perform competently and to take necessary steps to do so.

2.9 *Indemnity Insurance* – Psychotherapists are required to ensure that their professional work is adequately covered by appropriate indemnity insurance.

2.10 *Detrimental behaviour*

   i Psychotherapists are required to refrain from any behaviour that may be detrimental to the profession, to colleagues or to trainees.

  ii Psychotherapists are required to take appropriate action in accordance with Clause 5.7 with regard to the behaviour of a colleague which may be detrimental to the profession, to colleagues or to trainees.

# 3 Advertising

Member Organisations of UKCP are required to restrict promotion of their work to a description of the type of psychotherapy they provide.

Psychotherapists are required to distinguish carefully between self-descriptions, as in a list, and advertising seeking enquiries.

# 4 Code of Practice

Each Member Organisation of UKCP will have published a Code of Practice approved by the appropriate UKCP Section and appropriate for the practitioners of that particular organisation and their clients. The purpose of Codes of Practice is to clarify and expand upon the general principles established in the Code of Ethics of the organisation and the practical application of those principles. All psychotherapists on the UKCP Register will be required to adhere to the Codes of Practice of their own organisations.

# 5 Complaints procedure

Each Member Organisation of UKCP must have published a Complaints Procedure, including information about the acceptability or otherwise of a complaint made by a third party against a practitioner, approved by the appropriate UKCP Section and appropriate for the practitioners of that particular organisation and their clients. The purpose of a Complaints Procedure is to ensure that practitioners and their clients have clear information about the procedure and processes involved in dealing with complaints. All psychotherapists on the UKCP Register are required to adhere to the Complaints Procedure of their own organisations.

5.1 *Making a complaint* – A client wishing to complain shall be advised to contact the Member Organisation.

5.2 *Receiving a complaint* – A Member Organisation receiving a complaint against one of its psychotherapists shall ensure that the therapist is informed immediately and that both complainant and therapist are aware of the Complaints Procedure.

5.3 *Appeals*

i After the completion of the Complaints Procedure within an organisation, provision must be made for an appeal, stating time limits, grounds and procedures.

ii After the completion of all procedures in an organisation, an appeal may be made to the Section on grounds of improper procedure.

iii Reference to UKCP Governing Board – Appeals not resolved by the Section or those where the Section cannot appropriately hear the appeal shall be referred to the Governing Board of UKCP.

5.4 *Reports to UKCP Section* – Where a complaint is upheld the Section shall be informed by the organisation.

5.5 *Report to the UKCP Registration Board* – Member Organisations are required to report to the UKCP Registration Board the names of members who have been suspended or expelled.

5.6 *Complaints upheld and convictions* – Psychotherapists are required to inform their Member Organisations if any complaint is upheld against them in another Member Organisation, if they are convicted of any notifiable criminal offence or if successful civil proceedings are brought against them in relation to their work as psychotherapists.

5.7 *Conduct of colleagues* – Psychotherapists concerned that a colleague's conduct may be unprofessional should initiate the Complaints Procedure of the relevant Member Organisation.

5.8 The resignation of a member of an organisation shall not be allowed to impede the process of any investigation as long as the alleged offence took place during that person's membership.


## 6  Sanctions

Psychotherapists who are suspended by, or expelled from, a Member Organisation are automatically deleted from the UKCP Register.


## 7  Monitoring complaints

7.1 Member Organisations shall report to the Registration Board annually concerning the number of complaints received, the nature of the complaints and their disposition.

7.2 The Registration Board shall report annually to the Governing Board on the adequacy of Member Organisations' disciplinary procedures.

# Appendix 2

# Complaints procedures and protocols

## THE BRITISH ASSOCIATION FOR COUNSELLING

The Complaints Procedure can be used as a single-stage or two-stage procedure. It was written from the experience of using a similar procedure for five years and after considerable consultation with the Association's lawyers.

## 1    Introduction

### 1.1    Aim

The aim of this procedure is to afford protection to the public and to protect the name of the profession of counselling and psychotherapy as conducted by both individual and organisational members of the Association.

### 1.2    Bringing a complaint

A complaint can be brought either by a member of the public seeking or using a service provided by a member of the Association, or by a member of the Association themselves.

### 1.3    Complaints against non-members

The Association cannot deal with complaints against individuals or organisations who are not members of the Association.

*1.4   Procedure*

In outline the complaints procedure provides that:

On receipt of a complaint a decision will be made EITHER:

(a)   to accept the complaint for adjudication
OR
(b)   require the complaint to be remitted for preliminary investigation
OR
(c)   to reject the complaint.

The procedure requires that a complaint is correctly formulated and that enough information is available for a decision to be made as to whether the complaint should go forward to be adjudicated or not. In cases where the information is considered insufficient for adjudication the complaint may be sent for preliminary investigation. The facts discovered at preliminary investigation will inform the decision on whether the complaint should be accepted for adjudication or not. The adjudication of a complaint may be followed by the imposition of sanctions.

*1.5   Timescale*

1.5.1 A complaint shall be lodged within 5 years of the event(s) which form(s) the substance of that complaint.
1.5.2 All documentary records of complaints will be kept for a period of 2 years from the finalisation of the Complaints Procedure. Thereafter details of the formal complaint, adjudication, investigation, and appeal decisions and sanctions will be kept for a further 5 years.

*1.6   Administration*

The administration of the Complaints Procedure will follow protocols laid down from time to time by the Complaints Committee of the Association and these will be administered by the Clerk to the Complaints Committee and designated headquarters' staff.

*1.7   Expenses*

The Association is not responsible for travel or any other expenses incurred either by the Complainant or the Member Complained Against in connection with any stage of the complaint.

## 1.8   Preparatory consultations

Before making the complaint, the Complainant is expected to attempt to resolve the issue with the Individual or Organisational Member Complained Against. The Complainant must demonstrate that all informal channels or, in the case of organisational members, all internal channels have been exhausted. If they have not, the Complainant will need to explain or demonstrate why not.

Any person considering making a complaint may have preliminary discussions concerning the proper formulation of the complaint and the implementation of the Complaints Procedure with the Clerk to the Complaints Committee.

## 1.9   Dual accountability

The Association may decide to investigate or adjudicate a complaint against a member when another organisation is involved in a similar process arising out of the same substantive matters. Members of the Association have to accept that membership involves obligations, and these have to be considered in their own right.

## 2   Making a complaint

### 2.1 The complaint

The complaint must satisfy the following conditions:

(a)   the allegation is about a breach of a specific clause or clauses of any Code of Ethics and Practice of the Association

(b)   the complaint is brought either by a member of the public seeking or using a service provided by a member OR by a current member of the Association against another member of the Association

(c)   the individual or organisational Member Complained Against is named, AND is a current member of the Association AND was a member of the Association at the time of the alleged cause for complaint

(d)   a current member of the Association bringing a complaint must also have been a member of the Association at the time of the alleged cause for complaint

(e)   attempts to resolve the matter between the parties are shown to have been made or, if not, an explanation of why not is provided

(f)   legal proceedings have not been issued or contemplated regarding matters forming the subject matter of the complaint

(g)  the written and signed complaint is received by the Chief Executive of the Association.

## 2.2  *Acceptance of a complaint*

(a)  A copy of the complaint will be forwarded by the Chief Executive to the Chair of the Complaints Committee. A copy will also be forwarded to the Chair of the Standards and Ethics Committee for the Chair's comments.
(b)  The Complaints Committee will consider the complaint and any comment from the Chair of the Standards and Ethics Committee.
(c)  The Complaints Committee will decide whether to accept or reject the complaint, or decide that lack of sufficient information requires a preliminary investigation prior to making such a decision, in which case the procedure in section 3 will be followed.
(d)  Once the complaint is accepted the Clerk to the Complaints Committee will be asked by the Complaints Committee to start the formal Complaints Procedure.
(e)  If the complaint is rejected by the Complaints Committee, the Complaints Procedure will forthwith be terminated and the Complainant accordingly notified.

## 3  Preliminary Investigation

3.1.  When there is insufficient information contained in the complaint the Complaints Committee has the power under section 2.2.c to direct that preliminary investigation and reporting of facts to the Complaints Committee take place before a decision is made on whether or not the complaint shall proceed to adjudication.

3.2  Following the completion of the preliminary investigation the Complaints Committee shall decide whether or not the complaint shall be accepted and proceed to adjudication or be rejected.

## 3.3  *Preliminary investigation meeting*

The Chair of the Complaints Committee will appoint one or more independent persons (the Investigators), who will act impartially, to investigate and prepare a report on the complaint for the Complaints Committee. The Clerk to the Complaints Committee will make arrangements for the Investigator(s) to meet with the Complainant and the Member Complained Against, either separately or together, as soon as practicable.

## 3.4 Notice of meeting

The Clerk to the Complaints Committee will send written details of arrangements for the Preliminary Investigation meeting to the Complainant and the Member Complained Against.

## 3.5 Outcome

Following the meeting(s) the Investigator(s) will send a report to the Complaints Committee. The Preliminary Investigation report will be sent to the Complainant and the Member Complained Against who will be required to submit any response to the Complaints Committee within 14 days. After considering all submissions the Complaints Committee will decide whether or not the complaint should be accepted and proceed to adjudication or be rejected.

## 3.6 Failure to attend the Preliminary Investigation meeting

3.6.1 The refusal or failure of either the Complainant or the Member Complained Against to attend the Preliminary Investigation meeting without good reason or without at least 15 days notice will be notified to the Chair of the Complaints Committee. The Chair of the Complaints Committee may EITHER:

(a) terminate the Preliminary Investigation, which action may be published in the Association's Journal. This will bring the Complaints Procedure to an end.

OR

(b) rearrange the Preliminary Investigation meeting for a date not less than 28 days in advance

OR

(c) recommend to the Chair of the Association the termination of the membership of the Member Complained Against. If agreed the Chair of the Association will implement this action, notice of which will be published in the Association's Journal.

3.6.2 What constitutes good reason shall be solely at the discretion of the Chair of the Complaints Committee who will take advice on the matter from the Association's solicitor.

## 4 Appeals procedure following Preliminary Investigation

*4.1* Either party may appeal against a decision, not to proceed to adjudication following Preliminary Investigation, by writing to the Clerk to the Complaints Committee within 28 days of notification of the decision.

*4.2* The Chair of the Association will appoint up to three people not previously involved in the case to decide the appeal (the Investigation Appeal Panel). One member must be a member of the Management Committee of the Association.

*4.3* The Investigation Appeal Panel will review the evidence on which the decision of the Complaints Committee was made. The Investigation Appeal Panel may take advice on these papers from the Chair of the Standards and Ethics Committee and from the Association's Solicitor.

*4.4* The Investigation Appeal Panel will report its conclusions and recommendations to the Chair of the Association who will implement the Investigation Appeal Panel's decision which will be final.

*4.5* The decision of the Investigation Appeal Panel will be notified to the parties in writing within 14 days. No reasons shall be required to be appended to that decision.

## 5 The formal complaints procedure

### 5.1 Notification

Copies of the formal complaint will be forwarded to:

(a) the Individual or Organisational Member Complained Against
AND
(b) an Organisational Member of the Association of which the Individual Member Complained Against is known to be a member or is known to be currently working for.

### 5.2 Responding to a formal complaint

The Member Complained Against will be invited to submit a written response to the formal complaint to the Complaints Committee within 28 days.

## 5.3  Evidence

All evidence submitted by either the Complainant or the Member Complained Against will be open and available to all parties involved in the complaint. The Association will distribute to the other parties copies of all submissions made.

A person who is not a party to the complaint shall not be entitled to copies of any documentation which comes into the possession of the Association as a result of the complaint.

## 5.4  Conduct

Persons taking part in the Complaints Procedure are required to act in a manner that preserves confidentiality and avoids prejudicing the procedure's outcome or exercising an improper influence upon it. Any breach of this may result in the procedure being halted or terminated at any stage by the Chair of the Complaints Committee. The protocols on conduct will be as laid down and published by the Complaints Committee.

## 5.5  Suspension of rights of membership

The Chair of the Complaints Committee can, after consultation with the Chair of the Association, pending the completion of the adjudication, suspend the Member Complained Against's rights of membership of the Association when the complaint is of sufficient seriousness or because it alleges EITHER:

i   physical or emotional harm has been caused
AND/OR
ii   the exploitation of a member of the public is involved
AND/OR
iii   where the complaint is of such a kind that it could result in the expulsion of the individual or organisational member from the Association if the complaint is upheld.

In addition to or instead of the aforementioned the following rights of membership can be suspended with immediate effect:

(a)  promotion in publications of the Association
(b)  the occupancy of a role within any structures or affiliated groups of the Association
(c)  the right to put oneself forward for election to the Management

Committee, the Chair of a Committee or the Executive of a Division
(d) voting rights
(e) any professional status conferred by virtue of membership such as Accreditation and Registration
(f) the right of an organisational member to continue to sponsor members on to the United Kingdom Register of Counsellors.

The Chair of the Complaints Committee will notify the Member Complained Against of the suspension of membership or of the suspension of any rights of membership.

No liability for any loss suffered will attach to the Association for the suspension of membership or rights of membership even where a complaint is not upheld.

### 5.6 Lapsed membership

Failure to renew membership by a Member Complained Against during the course of a complaint shall not normally terminate the Complaints Procedure, which will continue to its conclusion. The Chair of the Complaints Committee may however recommend to the Chair of the Association that a failure to renew membership reflects circumstances which justify a termination of the procedure. Such a recommendation, if accepted, will require the approval of the Management Committee of the Association. The Chair of the Association will then implement that decision which will be published in the Association's Journal and notified to the parties.

## 6 The Adjudication procedure

### 6.1 Adjudication Panel

The Chair of the Complaints Committee will appoint a panel of not less than three persons to adjudicate the complaint (The Adjudication Panel) and to preside over the Adjudication meeting. The composition of the Adjudication Panel will have regard to the aims of the Complaints Procedure, and the requirement on Members of the Adjudication Panel to be impartial. It will also have regard to the Association's equal opportunity policies and to the need for expertise required by the substance of the complaint.

## 6.2 Purpose

The purpose of the Adjudication meeting is to examine complaints in a formal manner, decide on their validity and recommend sanctions as appropriate. Where there are several complaints against the same member they may be heard separately or at the same Adjudication meeting at the discretion of the Chair of the Complaints Committee.

## 6.3 Declaration of interest

Members of the Adjudication Panel have a duty to declare any interest which may be considered to compromise their impartiality. The views of the Complainant and the Member Complained Against will be taken into consideration when deciding whether the impartiality of any member of the Adjudication Panel might be so compromised as to require that they be replaced.

## 6.4 Venue

Adjudication meetings will be held at or within the vicinity of the Association's headquarters.

The venue selected for an Adjudication meeting will provide a secure and confidential environment.

## 6.5 Presence of a 'friend/support person'

When appearing at the Adjudication meeting, both the Complainant and the Member Complained Against may be accompanied by a 'friend' who may support and can represent them.

## 6.6 Conduct of meeting

The Chair of the Adjudication meeting (who shall be one of the Adjudication Panel) is responsible for ensuring that the Adjudication meeting is conducted in a manner which shows due regard to the gravity of the situation and to considerations of confidentiality.

The Adjudication meeting will be conducted in accordance with the protocols laid down by the Complaints Committee for the conduct of Adjudication meetings. These protocols will be made available to all parties at the time they are notified of the date and time of the Adjudication meeting.

## 6.7 Administration

The Clerk to the Complaints Committee is responsible for arranging the Adjudication meeting and notifying all parties in writing.

## 6.8 Written evidence

Written evidence and/or submissions and witness statements must be submitted in advance by the Complainant and the Member Complained Against. All evidence, submissions and witness statements will be open and available to all parties. Evidence, submissions and witness statements must be received by the Clerk to the Complaints Committee not less than 21 days prior to the date fixed for the Adjudication meeting. Such papers will be circulated to the Adjudication Panel, the Complainant and the Member Complained Against, not less than 14 days prior to the meeting. The Chair of the Adjudication meeting may take advice on these papers and/or procedural matters from the Association's solicitor.

## 6.9 New evidence

The only new evidence to be admitted on the day of the Adjudication meeting will be short oral or written submissions or otherwise solely at the discretion of the Chair of the Adjudication meeting.

## 6.10 Attendance by witnesses

The Adjudication Panel alone may invite witnesses to attend, to clarify and answer questions about their written statements.

## 6.11 Failure to attend the Adjudication meeting

6.11.1 The refusal or failure of either the Complainant or the Member Complained Against to attend the Adjudication meeting without 'good reason' or without at least 15 days' notice will be notified to the Chair of the Complaints Committee. The Chair of the Complaints Committee may EITHER:

(a)    terminate the Adjudication procedure which action may be published in the Association's Journal. This will bring the Complaints Procedure to an end.

OR

(b)    rearrange the Adjudication meeting for a date not less than 28 days in advance

OR

(c)    recommend to the Chair of the Association the termination of the membership of the Member Complained Against. If agreed the Chair of the Association will implement this action notice of which will be published in the Association's Journal.

6.11.2 What constitutes 'good reason' shall be solely at the discretion of the Chair of the Complaints Committee who will take advice on the matter from the Association's Solicitor.

## 6.12   *The Adjudication*

Following the conclusion of the Adjudication meeting the Adjudication Panel will decide whether the complaint is proved or not and may make recommendations on sanctions to be imposed. The Adjudication Panel will within 28 days report its decision in writing to the Chair of the Complaints Committee. In the light of the decision the Complaints Committee will thereafter decide upon the sanctions that it proposes to recommend to the Chair of the Association to impose in accordance with section 6.13.iii.

## 6.13   *Notification of findings*

i    Within 28 days the decision of the Adjudication Panel will be notified to the Chair of the Complaints Committee, the Complainant and the Member Complained Against by the Chair of the Complaints Committee (the notification of sanctions will be made as in (iv) below).

ii    The Chair of the Complaints Committee will notify the decision of the Adjudication Panel to the Chair of the Association.

iii    The Chair of the Complaints Committee will forward the recommendations of the Complaints Committee regarding sanctions to be imposed, to the Chair of the Association who will decide thereafter on the sanctions to be imposed.

iv    The Member Complained Against will be notified of any sanctions imposed by the Chair of the Association.

v    The decision to uphold a complaint will be published, detailing the clauses held to have been breached, in the Association's Journal. Any sanctions imposed will be published in the

Association's Journal. The publication of decision and sanctions
will be made only after the necessary time for notification of
appeal has elapsed. (See Section 8.)

vi   In a case where the individual Member Complained Against is a
member of or is known to be currently working for an Organisational Member of the Association, the Organisational Member
will be informed of the outcome of the Complaints Procedure.

## 7   Sanctions

Any of the following sanctions may be imposed:

i     requirement to demonstrate specified change/improvement by a
specific date
ii    provision of reports from a supervisor, acceptable to the Association, appointed to monitor the member's work
iii   suspension of any professional status conferred by virtue of membership such as Accreditation or Registration and/or membership
rights for a specific period and/or until conditions specified by the
Association have been satisfied
iv    termination of any professional status or membership
v     a directive to cease counselling/training/supervision or other counselling related activities for a specific period or indefinitely
vi    such other sanctions as may from time to time be appropriate to the
particular circumstances of a case.

### 7.1  Lifting of sanctions

The Member Complained Against may make application to the Chair
of the Complaints Committee for the lifting of sanctions when the conditions laid down in the sanctions have been fulfilled. The Complaints
Committee will consider the evidence of compliance and will recommend to the Chair of the Association whether or not sanctions should be
lifted. The Chair of the Association will notify the member of the
decision. The lifting of sanctions will be published in the Association's
Journal.

### 7.2  Failure to comply with sanctions

Failure to comply with sanctions will result in the Chair of the
Complaints Committee writing to the Chair of the Association with

information and recommendations on whether or not to terminate membership. The Chair of the Association will notify the member of the decision of the Management Committee which may be published in the Association's Journal.

## 8    Appeals procedure following Adjudication

*8.1* The Member Complained Against may appeal against the decision and/or the sanction(s) by writing to the Clerk to the Complaints Committee within 28 days of the notification of the sanctions.

*8.2* The Chair of the Association will appoint up to three people not previously involved in the case, to decide the appeal (the Adjudication Appeal Panel). One member must be a member of the Management Committee of the Association.

*8.3* The Adjudication Appeal Panel will review the evidence on which the Adjudication Panel's decision was made, its decision and the sanctions imposed. The Adjudication Appeal Panel can at its discretion interview the Member Complained Against and the Complainant who shall both be entitled to bring a 'friend' to that interview who may support and represent them.

*8.4* The Adjudication Appeal Panel will report its decision to the Management Committee which will implement its decision which will be final.

*8.5* The decision of the Adjudication Appeal Panel will be notified to the parties in writing within 14 days. No reasons shall be required to be appended to that decision.

*8.6* Where the appeal is not allowed the original decisions of the Adjudication Panel and the sanctions imposed by the Chair of the Association will be published in the Association's Journal.

## 9    Publication

*9.1* The Association reserves the right to publish such details of complaints as it considers appropriate.

*9.2* Any notification that the Association, under these procedures, is entitled to publish in its Journal may, at its discretion, be published elsewhere by the Association.

*9.3* The termination of membership under the Complaints Procedure will be reported in the Association's Journal.

## 10   Effective date

*10.1* This Complaints Procedure will apply to all complaints presented
to the Association after 1 November 1997. Complaints presented prior to
1 November 1997 will be dealt with under the Complaints Procedure
then existing.

## THE BRITISH CONFEDERATION OF PSYCHOTHERAPISTS

This is an umbrella organization and its guidelines for members are set
out in 'The British Confederation of Psychotherapists, Standards for
Codes of Ethics of Member Organisations'. These require members
under their Constitution and Guidelines for Membership Part II A and B
to have complaints procedures and disciplinary procedures. The BCP
has an appeals process on the grounds of failure to follow procedure.

## THE BRITISH PSYCHOLOGICAL SOCIETY

The documents below are particularly helpful because they respond to
the needs of the complainant *and* the practitioner.

## HOW TO COMPLAIN ABOUT A MEMBER OF THE SOCIETY

If you believe that a member of the Society may be guilty of professional
misconduct, you have the right to complain. All Chartered Psychologists
are members of The British Psychological Society.

The following notes tell you how to make a complaint.

### The complaint

If you believe that a member of this Society may be liable to disciplinary
action then all that you have to do is send a complaint to the Society's
Honorary General Secretary.

The complaint must be in writing and it should be accompanied by a
complete account of the relevant facts.

You should be aware that none of the Society's disciplinary procedures
stop you from taking legal action in the courts in the usual way.

## Committees concerned with your complaint

There will be several stages in the consideration of your complaint. It may go to some or all of the following committees:

*The Investigatory Committee* – Four psychologists serve on this Committee: the President of the Society, the Honorary General Secretary, and two other senior officers.

*An Investigation Panel* – may be set up by the Investigatory Committee to investigate your complaint. It will consist of two to five senior members of the Society with relevant experience.

A *Disciplinary Committee* – may be appointed on which two distinguished lay members of the public (that is people who are not themselves psychologists) will serve along with one psychologist who will be a past President of the Society. These three people are drawn from the membership of the Disciplinary Board.

*The Disciplinary Board* – Ten people sit on this Board: six lay members of the public and four past Presidents of the Society. The Disciplinary Board meets only once a year.

*The Chair of the Disciplinary Board* – is always a lay member of the public and never a psychologist. No complaint can be dismissed without the agreement of the Chair of the Disciplinary Board (or one of the other lay members of the Board standing in for him or her).

A senior member of the office staff of the Society serves as Clerk to the Investigatory Committee and Disciplinary Board. The Clerk will advise on procedure, make arrangements for hearings, answer queries and communicate with the complainant and the accused member.

## What happens when your complaint is received?

Your letter will be acknowledged and then passed to the Investigatory Committee.

This Committee may decide to:

- set up an Investigatory Panel to consider the allegation further;
- recommend to the Chair of the Disciplinary Board, or other non-psychologist member of the Disciplinary Board standing in, that the complaint is dismissed. The complaint will be dismissed if it does not fall within the scope of the Society's disciplinary responsibilities for professional misconduct. The Society will only investigate complaints that relate to and/or affect the member's work as a psychologist. Before any decision is reached you may be asked to provide more information or to clarify the nature of your complaint.

If the Investigatory Committee decides to recommend that the complaint be dismissed, this recommendation and the complaint is considered, totally independently, by the non-psychologist Chair of the Disciplinary Board or other lay member of the Disciplinary Board standing in.

The Disciplinary Board Representative can overrule the recommendation and can decide instead to set up an Investigatory Panel.

When an Investigatory Panel is set up, you may be asked to provide more information, or to give more details. Usually the member against whom the complaint has been made will be asked for information and given the chance to comment on the complaint.

When an Investigatory Panel has completed its work, it reports back to the Investigatory Committee. This Committee decides:

- that a Disciplinary Committee must be set up to hear the allegations and conduct a hearing rather like a court;
- or to recommend to the Chair of the Disciplinary Board that the complaint should be dismissed;
- or to recommend to the Chair of the Disciplinary Board or other non-psychologist member of the Disciplinary Board standing in, that he or she authorise the Investigatory Committee to write to the subject of the complaint and, when reporting that the matter will not be referred to a Disciplinary Committee, may advise in relation to the Code of Conduct.

If the Investigatory Committee, on the basis of the report from an Investigatory Panel, decides to recommend that the complaint be dismissed or to make comment, then the recommendation and all the information is reconsidered, totally independently, by the non-psychologist Disciplinary Board Representative. The Disciplinary Board Representative again has the authority to overrule the recommendation and can instead require either that the complaint be investigated further or that a Disciplinary Committee be appointed.

If the accused member does not accept any comment made by the Investigatory Committee, he or she can request that the matter be referred to the Disciplinary Committee.

When a Disciplinary Committee is appointed it will conduct a hearing rather like a court. As the complainant, you may be called to be a witness and you may be questioned on the allegation either by the accused or solicitors or a representative acting for the accused. Other witnesses may also be called and questioned.

## The outcome

The Disciplinary Committee will find the accused guilty or not guilty of professional misconduct. If the member is judged to be guilty of professional misconduct various sanctions are available ranging from reprimanding the member through to removal from the Register of Chartered Psychologists and expulsion from the Society.

The outcome may be reported to the press but normally your identity will not be disclosed without your consent. Disciplinary Committee hearings are not open to the public or the press.

In all cases, whatever the decision, you will be notified of the outcome.

## Some other things you should know

The full investigation of a complaint from the time of the first allegation may take many months to resolve. All the people involved in investigating the complaint are either senior, volunteer members of the Society or distinguished lay members of the public who are having to fit in their voluntary work for the Society with numerous other commitments.

The Society's procedures for investigating complaints about its members are laid down in its Royal Charter and Statutes. Copies of the Charter and Statutes can be provided free of charge but if you have any queries about how to make your complaint or about the course of an investigation you are advised to consult the Clerk at the Society's Leicester office.

Finally, it is important to remind potential complainants that the Society can investigate complaints only if the psychologist concerned is a member of the Society. For this reason the Society advises members of the public to consult only Chartered Psychologists. Chartered psychologists and all other members of the Society have agreed to adhere to a Code of Conduct, a copy of which is enclosed.

To complain about a member of the Society write to:

Honorary General Secretary
The British Psychological Society
St Andrews House
48 Princess Road East
LEICESTER LE1 7DR
Telephone: 0116 254 9568

(Published by The British Psychological Society, 1994.)

## HOW TO ENDURE A COMPLAINT ABOUT YOUR CONDUCT

Under the terms of its Royal Charter, the Society is required to investigate complaints about members. When a member of the public or another psychologist wishes to make a complaint about a member, they are sent a copy of the attached information sheet 'How to complain . . . '.

As the Register of Chartered Psychologists becomes widely known, it is expected that there will be an increase in the number of complaints. All categories of member are subject to the complaints procedures. In some cases these will be trivial or irrelevant. The Society's complaints procedure is concerned only with professional misconduct.

Nobody welcomes having a complaint made against them but an essential aspect of the Register of Chartered Psychologists is that those on the Register are publicly accountable for their actions as psychologists through disciplinary procedures which involve lay members. These notes provide some guidance on how to endure a complaint.


### What happens after a complaint is received?

All letters containing allegations are considered by the Investigatory Committee. If a decision is reached that investigation of the allegation is not justified, then the Committee seeks the approval of the Chair of the Disciplinary Board or a nominated non-psychologist member of the Disciplinary Board not to pursue the complaint. If the Disciplinary Board Representative agrees, you, the member, are usually informed about the complaint and the decision not to investigate it.

Occasionally you will not be informed; when, for instance, the complaint has nothing to do with your position as a psychologist, or it appears that the complainant has picked the member about whom to complain by chance.

If the Investigatory Committee decides that the complaint must be investigated, then an Investigatory Panel will be appointed. The Investigatory Panel comprises between two and five Fellows of the Society. The task of the Panel is to establish the facts and investigate the complaint. Sometimes the Panel will need to confer with the complainant or interview other people before you are alerted to the complaint in a letter of notification. Even if the Panel comes to the conclusion that the complaint is groundless, you will usually be notified. Statute 14(7) requires 'that the Panel must be satisfied that the person against whom the allegation is made has been given the opportunity of making written representation to it'. You have no right to require a face to face interview with the Panel, though at the Panel's discretion an opportunity may be given for you to be heard in person.

It should be remembered that at this stage, you have not been 'charged' with professional misconduct. You have simply been notified of a complaint and asked to give your account of the issue. Experience has shown that many complaints turn out to be either groundless, or too trivial to pursue further; you may have been guilty of no more than poor judgement or sloppy work practices. In these circumstances the investigatory process, or the knowledge that a complaint has been made, may cause you to review your behaviour. Having carried out its investigation, the Panel has to report to the Investigatory Committee. Usually this report will contain recommendations, but it is the responsibility of the Committee to decide to:

- take no further action;
- recommend to the Chair of the Disciplinary Board or other non-psychologist member of the Disciplinary Board standing in, that he or she authorise the Investigatory Committee to write to the subject of the complaint and, when reporting that the matter will not be referred to a Disciplinary Committee, may advise in relation to the Code of Conduct;
- refer the complaint to a Disciplinary Committee.

In the case of 'no action' the Disciplinary Board representative will again be asked to agree and you will be informed. The complainant will also be notified of the outcome at this stage.

In a minority of cases, the Investigatory Committee will conclude that there is sufficient evidence of professional misconduct and that the allegation must be considered by a Disciplinary Committee. When this happens a Disciplinary Committee will be appointed consisting of three members of the Disciplinary Board, two lay members and one psychologist who is a past President of the Society. The Disciplinary Committee may be advised by a lawyer, and up to two Fellows of the Society with special expertise in the matter under investigation. These advisers may only give guidance to the Committee (and only at its request); they do not share in the judgement.

Either a member of the Investigatory Committee or of the Panel that investigated the allegation will be appointed to present to the Disciplinary Committee such information as is available and relevant. You will then be given a full and fair opportunity to be heard and to call witnesses and cross-examine any other witnesses. In other words the proceedings of the Disciplinary Committee will be similar to those of a court. You are allowed either to conduct your own case, or to be represented by a lawyer, or by another person of your choice (e.g. a trade union official or friend). Written evidence may be submitted by both yourself and the Investigatory Committee. The Disciplinary Committee then has to decide whether or not you are guilty of professional misconduct.

The Disciplinary Committee is guided by Article 12 of the Charter and by the Code of Conduct but, in the words of Statute 15(12), 'the mention or lack of mention in the Code of Conduct of a particular act or omission shall not be taken as conclusive on any question of professional misconduct'. This is because no Code of Conduct could ever anticipate every possible offence that might be committed.

If the Disciplinary Committee finds someone guilty, one or more of the following actions may be taken:

- the member may be reprimanded or severely reprimanded;
- the member may be requested to give an undertaking to refrain from continuing or repeating the offending conduct;
- the member may be suspended from the Society or the Register or both for a period not greater than two years;
- the member may be expelled from the Society, removed from the Register or both.

## Making the decision public

The decision of the Disciplinary Committee will be sent to you by the Clerk to the Committee. The Disciplinary Committee also has authority to publish the names of those disciplined, reporting that a named member had been reprimanded or struck off the Register and that the public should note that this person is no longer in good standing within the profession.

## The Clerk

The Statutes provide for members of the office staff to serve as Clerks to the Investigatory Committee and the Disciplinary Committee. Their role is to advise these committees on procedure, make the arrangements for hearings and communicate with the accused member as a neutral 'broker'. Where an accused member wants advice on his or her 'rights' or has any other queries regarding the investigatory or disciplinary process, the Clerk is the person to approach in confidence.

## How complaints are initiated

Most complaints start with an accusation of professional misconduct raised by a member of the public (usually a client of a psychologist) or by a colleague who is acting under the provisions of Clause 5.10 of the Code of Conduct which requires psychologists who suspect misconduct by a professional colleague to bring that misconduct to the attention of those charged with responsibility to investigate it.

However, the Society's solicitors have advised that the Investigatory Committee itself or a member of it can have a duty to the public to initiate the investigatory process. For instance, the Society would probably have to take action if a newspaper carried reports about the alleged professional misconduct of a member that had not been reported directly to the Honorary General Secretary. Members need not fear that the Society will initiate 'witch hunts' but from time to time it will have to act on third party information in order to protect the public.

## Confidentiality of proceedings

Up to the end of the disciplinary process the proceedings are confidential. The Disciplinary Committee meets in camera because sometimes the complaint will require the disclosure of sensitive personal information about clients. Confidentiality is also a means of protecting the interests of a member who is found to be in need of help. However, the primary responsibility of the Disciplinary Committee is to serve the interests of the public and this will usually mean publishing the names of those who have been disciplined.

Unfortunately, confidentiality is something that can never be guaranteed. Vengeful clients may inform the press that they have made a complaint or the alleged misconduct may have been the subject of widespread rumour or report in the media.

Because of this, the Society has adopted the practice of agreeing with the Chair of the Disciplinary Board a form of words that can be used if the Society is approached to comment on a matter that has been investigated.

When an allegation is still under investigation any enquirers will be told that the matter is 'sub judice' and therefore no comment can be made. However, once a decision has been made 'not to pursue' a complaint or a member has been found 'not guilty' a form of words such as 'the member was exonerated' or 'there was no basis on which to pursue the allegations' will be agreed. Sometimes, the member who has been accused may wish the Society to release a statement 'to clear his or her name'. In other circumstances a different person from the original complainant may bring to the Society's attention the same accusation, in which case the agreed form of words would be used.

At the end of each year the Disciplinary Board holds an annual review meeting. One goal for the future is that the Society should publish the outcomes of certain enquiries as a means of drawing members' attention to matters of principle or pitfalls to be avoided. The identities of the actual members involved will, of course, be disguised.

## A disclaimer

These notes have been prepared as information for members facing allegations about their professional conduct. They cannot however be taken as binding on the Society or its officers and officials. The Society's Royal Charter and Statutes must be referred to as the authoritative account of the investigatory and disciplinary procedures to which these notes refer.

(Published by The British Psychological Society, 1994.)

## THE UNITED KINGDOM COUNCIL FOR PSYCHOTHERAPY

The UKCP is also an umbrella organization and its Complaints Procedure provides a template for its members. This procedure is under revision.

Complaints will normally be received by:

- the member organization to which the registered *psychotherapist* belongs,

*or by*

- the UKCP itself if the complaint is against a member organization a Section or part of UKCP. UKCP can deal only with matters relating to *registered psychotherapists or member organizations.*

## 1    Role of organizations

### *1.1    General considerations*

The informal and formal process of an internal complaints procedure may be followed by an appeal and/or litigation, although this has not yet happened in this country. It is therefore advisable to keep accurate, detailed, written records of all proceedings, correspondence and telephone calls.

If a complaint is taken to court, there are several Acts that may be relevant e.g. Data Protection Act, Consumer Protection Act, Contract Law. Where a specific written contract with a trainee or client/patient has been made, this will be the measure against which the case will be heard. However the written contract will not be allowed to contravene the principles of natural justice which are as follows.

There must be a disciplined effort to be fair,

therefore:  clauses must be reasonable

clauses must comply with the law

exclusion or limitation of liability must be reasonable:

If there is no written contract or where it is not explicit the judge will decide what is reasonable. It is therefore in the Psychotherapist's or the member organisation's interest to be explicit while keeping contracts precise. Reference may be made to other documents, e.g. a Section flag statement or training brochure.

Hearing complaints – In order to protect the hearers of complaints, the complainants and the complained against, it is important that the insurers be informed as soon as a complaint is to be investigated. Insurers will bring in legal advice when and as it is needed. Organizations should seek legal advice in order to protect members of investigating and adjudicating panels.

It is important to respect a complaint and take it seriously. The limits of responsibility of members of all panels must be clearly stated in order to protect them and the complainant.

## 1.2    The principles of a Complaints Procedure

All Member Organizations of UKCP are required to have a complaints procedure which incorporates the following principles:

### 1.2.1   Accountability

Accountability of the Ethics Committee should be clear, e.g. via the Chair of the Management Committee to the Council, Trustees or members of the Organization.

### 1.2.2 Composition

The Ethics Committee should consist of senior members of the organization.

### 1.2.3 Cooption

Cooption of external advisers should be considered as part of good practice.

### 1.2.4 Procedures

There should be provision to ensure that informal attempts at resolution or conciliation have been exhausted.

(a) Procedures for receiving and responding to a complaint and preliminary considerations of whether there is a case to answer should be laid down and consistent.

(b) Procedures for dealing with a complaint should be clear. If there is a case to answer an investigating panel should be appointed. Investigating members should investigate facts, and seek to conciliate at the preliminary stage.

If conciliation is not possible an adjudicating panel should be appointed to determine the outcome. The adjudicating panel should not include members of the investigating panel.

### 1.2.5 Costs

Permission should be given for the investigating panel to seek expert advice at the cost of the Organization. Organizations need to be prepared for the cost of expert advice if necessary and need to consider who will bear all the costs.

### 1.2.6 Protocol

(a) Protocol before the Hearing should be set out.

(b) Protocol for the conduct of the Hearing should be set out.

(c) There should be a protocol for decision-making and methods of communicating outcomes and decisions.

1.2.7   Time limits

A time limit within which complaints may be brought (usually three years) should be specified. There should be time limits for each stage of the Hearing. It is useful to include the word 'Normally'. All parties involved should be kept appropriately informed at each stage of the process.

1.2.8   Sanctions

The range of sanctions and conditions which may be imposed should be clearly stated. Serious professional misconduct should be defined and should lead to loss of UKCP registration.

1.2.9   Appeals procedure

The Appeal Panel should be made up of a number of people who have had no previous involvement in the hearing.

1.2.10  Removal of sanctions

Conditions and time boundaries for removal of sanctions should be clearly stated.

1.2.11  Reporting

There should be a final report on the proceedings for each party involved in the complaint although there may be separate reports because of the need for confidentiality. The complaints procedure must also state the organization's responsibility for reporting complaints to other bodies, e.g. UKCP.

*1.3    Procedure after a complaint has been heard*

1.3.1   All complaints will be dealt with by the member organizations where that is relevant. Complaints received by the UKCP, the Registration Board or the Section concerned will be handled by the Chair of the Registration Board, who will pass such complaints on to the member organization responsible for the *psychotherapist* complained about.

1.3.2   A complainant who believes that a complaint has not been fairly or fully investigated may appeal against the procedure of the investigation to the Section and, if appealing against or complaining about the Section, may appeal to the Governing Board. Neither the Board nor the Section can consider the substance of the original complaint. However if a Section or the Board has reason to believe that a complaint has not been adequately or properly investigated it can require the organization to reinvestigate the complaint.

1.3.3    The organization must inform the Registration Board within 28 days of any registered *psychotherapist* who has been suspended or struck off. On receipt of this information the Board will contact the registered *psychotherapist*, informing of the right of appeal to the Section. The registered *psychotherapist* will be informed that he/she will be suspended unless making an appeal, and will be told whether the suspension will be temporary or whether he/she will be struck off the Register. The registered *psychotherapist* will be given a further 28 days to lodge an appeal and to inform the Registration Board that an appeal has been lodged. At the end of this time, if no notice of appeal has been received, the registered *psychotherapist's* name will be included on a monthly bulletin of changes to the register, as having been suspended or struck off the register.

1.3.4    Should the registered *psychotherapist* be shown in the Register as being a member of several organizations, the Board will write separately to the Disciplinary Committee of each of these organizations informing them that their member has been suspended or their name struck off.

### 1.3.5    Criminal offence

If a psychotherapist is convicted of a notifiable criminal offence he/she must report it to the disciplinary committee of the organization to which he/she belongs. The disciplinary committee must report the offence and its nature to the Registration Board which will decide whether temporary suspension from the Register is necessary pending a recommendation from the organization as to whether the psychotherapist should be struck off, suspended or whether no action should be taken.

## 2    Role of the Sections

### 2.1 Role of the Sections in dealing with appeals

A person involved in a complaint who considers that an organization has not satisfactorily dealt with it may appeal to the Section within 28 days of receiving the final report of the outcome of the complaint on the grounds that the organization has not followed due procedure.

*2.2* In practice such persons will normally either be:

1 the original complainant;
2 a *psychotherapist* against whom the complaint was made; or
3 a member of the disciplinary committee which dealt with the complaint.

*2.3* The Section, on receipt of a written appeal alleging improper procedure, will follow its own appeals procedure. Each Section must publish an appeals procedure. An appellant who is dissatisfied with the Section's manner of handling the case, may appeal to the Governing Board on the grounds that the Section has not followed due procedure. The Governing Board will appoint a committee to investigate such an appeal.

*2.4* In the event that the appeal is upheld by the Section, the Section shall require the organization to reinvestigate the complaint. In the event that an appeal is upheld by the Governing Board, the Section and/or organization will be required to reinvestigate the appeal. Failure to investigate or to reinvestigate according to the procedures of the organization or Section may result in disciplinary action against the organization or Section. In the last resort, this may result in a recommendation to the Governing Board and to the Council that the organization or Section be suspended from membership of the UKCP.

## *2.5 Monitoring the complaints process*

The Sections must monitor the complaints procedures of their constituent organizations. They must ensure that each of their member organizations has a complaints procedure which is consistent with any guidelines published by the Governing Board on behalf of UKCP.

*2.6* Failure to follow the UKCP Guidelines, or to put them into practice in the investigation of a particular complaint, would itself be a cause for legitimate appeal to the Section or, if against the Section, to the Governing Board.

*2.7* In addition, the Registration Board may institute an audit of complaints, and the manner of dealing with them. In pursuance of this, the Board may from time to time request Sections to provide information from one or more of their member organizations showing how many complaints have been received over a certain period, and how the organization has dealt with them up to the time of the report.

*2.8* Sections may from time to time receive complaints against member organizations. Each Section must have and publish a procedure for dealing with such complaints. If such a complaint is not resolved the Section may recommend to the Governing Board that the organization be suspended from membership of UKCP. Conditions and time limits for possible reinstatement must be specified. Appeal against a Section's adjudication of this sort will be to the Governing Board. Sections must inform the Registration Board and Governing Board of the suspension of any member organization.

### 3  Role of the Registration Board

*3.1* Each member organization is required to inform the relevant Section of the numbers of complaints received, the type of complaints, and their determination during each year ending on the last day of September.

*3.2* Each Section is required to inform the Registration Board of the cumulated statistics of the numbers of complaints and appeals received, the type of complaint or appeal, and their determination from each of their member organizations and, in addition, the same information on any complaints about organizations or about the Section received by the Section. These statistics are required to be in the hands of the Registration Board on the last day of October in each year.

*3.3* The Registration Board is presently required to report to the AGM on the number of complaints against registered *psychotherapists* and their outcome during the year preceding the AGM. These data are vital to enable UKCP to identify training shortfalls, the need for more ethical training or guidance, and the adequacy of the training provided by member organizations.

## GUIDELINES FOR PROTOCOLS

These are a few of the author's suggestions towards developing protocols for meetings.

### Investigation

*The aims of the meeting*

The aims might include:

1 the gathering of information;
2 the preparation of a report for the complaints committee which will inform any future hearing or process.

*The investigator*

The investigator should be a person of stature within the organization or from outside the organization who has no direct therapeutic or supervisory contact with any of the parties concerned in the complaint.

*The management of the meeting*

Arrangements to be made before the meeting:

- The *time* should, if possible, be mutually agreed. This can be difficult to arrange and it may be necessary instead to have the time set by the complaints committee.
- The *place* should be neutral, possibly the offices of the organization.
- *Submission of papers* and the number of copies that must be submitted within the prescribed time, according to the complaints procedure. The investigators would not normally accept papers submitted or tabled at the meeting.
- Whether the accompanying *'friend'* is acceptable and may or may not represent the complainant or practitioner.

The committee needs to decide whether:

- *the parties* are to be interviewed separately or together;
- there are limits placed on the *behaviour* of the parties;
- a statement about the committee's views and rulings on the *confidential* status of papers, submissions, what is said in the meeting and the report needs to be made;

- *transcripts* are to be prepared and whether they or *tapes* are to be made available to the parties.

At the meeting:

- *The general management* of the meeting. Water and possibly other refreshments need to be available for all of the parties. Refreshments will also be needed for the investigator and the person clerking the meeting. There need to be rooms available for people to wait and people around to manage the occasion. The microphone for tape recording, or the person taking verbatim shorthand, needs to be placed where all parties can be heard clearly.
- *Timing* – equal time needs to be given to both parties.

### The Report

*Each count or clause of the Code of Ethics and Practice should be considered separately*, and

- the areas of agreement about facts and understanding between the parties stated;
- the areas of disagreement about facts and understanding between the parties stated;
- a comment from the investigator about 'whether there may be a case to answer' or not on each count or clause;
- a comment from the investigator about whether there is no basis on which to proceed on each count or clause.

## Adjudication

### The aims of the meeting

The aims might include:

1 The gathering of information;
2 the preparation of a report for the complaints committee which will inform any future hearing or process.

### The adjudicators

The adjudicators should be people of stature within the organization and possibly one person from outside the organization who has no direct therapeutic or supervisory contact with either of the parties concerned in the complaint. They should reflect the parties in all matters to do with equal opportunities. Either the complaints committee or the panel itself needs to appoint a chair for the meeting and to hold responsibility for producing the panel's report.

### The conduct and management of the meeting

Before the meeting:

- The *time* should, if possible, be mutually agreed. This can be difficult and it may be necessary to have the time set by the complaints committee.
- The *place* where the meeting is held should be formal. It could be a neutral place or could be the offices of the organization.
- *Papers* must be submitted within the prescribed time, according to the complaints procedure. The adjudicators will need to read the papers on receipt and may wish for further information to be sought and/or to call witnesses. There needs to be guidance on papers submitted or tabled at the meeting with the adjudicators.

The committee needs to decide whether:

- there are limits placed on the *behaviour* of the parties, what they mean to do should anyone become very abusive;
- a statement needs to be made about the committee's views and rulings on the *confidential* status of papers, submissions, what is said in the meeting and the report;
- *transcripts* are to be prepared, and decisions taken whether they or *tapes* are to be made available to the parties.

At the meeting:

- *The setting and general management* – water and possibly other refreshments need to be available for all the parties, refreshments will also be needed for the investigator and the person clerking the meeting. There need to be rooms available for people to wait and a number of people on hand to receive, escort and do what is necessary.
- *Recording* – whether the meeting is to be verbatim recorded by someone taking shorthand or whether it is to be tape recorded, arrangements need to be made. Following the meeting, transcripts will need to be prepared or tapes made available for each of the parties.
- Normally *the parties are seen together.*

- *Timing* – time needs to be available for the adjudicators to consider the documents submitted before the meeting and for reflection after the formal meeting. Equal time must be given to both parties. The chair of the panel needs to manage time in the meeting.
- *Questioning* – all questions or comments should be put through the Chair.

The Chair outlines the situation.

The complainant puts questions to the practitioner.

The practitioner puts questions to the complainant.

Witnesses are called by either party. If the witness is called by the complainant, the complainant first questions the witness, then the practitioner does so. If the witness is called by the practitioner, the practitioner first questions the witness then the complainant does so.

The panel may then seek further clarification.

The Chair may ask the parties to summarize the situation or may do so him or herself. If the Chair summarizes then each party should be allowed to respond.

The Chair consults the panel to see that the members believe they have all the information they need.

The Chair closes the meeting.

## *The Report*

*Each count or clause of the Code of Ethics and Practice should be considered separately,* and a view stated by the adjudicators about whether they find that there has been a breach of the Codes or not.

Sanctions may be considered and recommended to the complaints committee.

# Appendix 3

# Letters

This appendix gives guidelines for writing letters and also some examples that you may wish to modify for your own use.

## GUIDELINES FOR WRITING LETTERS

1 Letters should have a formal tone and language to all parties.
2 Incoming letters should always be acknowledged soon after receipt even if there is nothing else to say.
3 Letters should be as brief as possible.
4 Letters should inform the receiver when to expect to hear from you next.
5 Letters and envelopes should be marked 'confidential' if you wish them to remain confidential.

**A letter to someone inquiring about the complaints procedure or code of ethics and practice**

Society of Independent Practitioners, 3 Roundway House
Leicester LE5 6BA

date

Dear John Smith,

Thank you for your letter of _____ . I am enclosing a copy of our Code of Ethics and Practice and our Complaints Procedure as requested.

Should you need further assistance please contact me through Mrs Sing at the above office/at my home address, Rose House, 6 Corner Lane, London W10 5BC.

Yours sincerely,


Ann Paul
Chair of the Complaints Committee



**Letters on receiving a complaint**

*To the complainant*

Society of Independent Practitioners, 3 Roundway House
Leicester LE5 6BA

Confidential

Please contact me at
Rose House
6 Corner Lane
London W10 5BC

date

Dear John Smith,

I have received your letter dated _____ enclosing your complaint against _____ , who is a member of this organization.

The Complaints Committee will discuss it at its meeting on _____ , and I will inform you within a week of its decision.

Matters of this kind are dealt with by the Society in the strictest confidence and I would ask you to maintain confidentiality on your own part. Failure to do so could threaten the livelihood of our member and might result in the complaint not being able to be pursued by the Society – see point x of our Complaints Procedure.

Yours sincerely,


Ann Paul
Chair of the Complaints Committee
enc. Complaints Procedure


*Letter to the member complained against*

Society of Independent Practitioners, 3 Roundway House
Leicester LE5 6BA

Confidential

Please contact me at
Rose House
6 Corner Lane
London W10 5BC                                                    date

Dear Barbara West,

We have received a complaint from John Smith a copy of which is attached for you to see. He alleges breaches of the Codes of Ethics and Practice of this Society. You will have copies of the Codes of Ethics and Practice and the Complaints Procedure in your procedures file of the Society. Should you need a further copy do telephone the office.

The Complaints Committee will discuss this complaint at its meeting on ——— , and I will inform you within a week of its decision to accept it or not.

I do not need to remind you that matters of this kind are dealt with in the strictest confidence and I would ask you to maintain confidentiality on your own part – see 5.2 of the Complaints Procedure. We would suggest that you get in touch with your supervisor/consultant and discuss the matter with him/her.

Yours sincerely,


Ann Paul
Chair of the Complaints Committee

**Letters informing both parties of the outcome of the meeting to decide whether the complaint is accepted or not**

*Non-acceptance*

Society of Independent Practitioners, 3 Roundway House
Leicester LE5 6BA

Confidential

Please contact me at
Rose House
6 Corner Lane
London W10 5BC                                              date

Dear John Smith,

The Complaints Committee of the Society met on ——— and has not accepted your complaint against Barbara West.

Should you wish to appeal against this decision you should do so within a month of this date.

Yours sincerely,


Ann Paul
Chair of the Complaints Committee

Society of Independent Practitioners, 3 Roundway House
Leicester LE5 6BA

Confidential

Please contact me at
Rose House
6 Corner Lane
London W10 5BC                                              date

Dear Barbara West,

The Complaints Committee of the Society met on ——— and has not accepted the complaint made by John Smith against you. John Smith has one month from this date to appeal against this decision.

Yours sincerely,


Ann Paul
Chair of the Complaints Committee

## Acceptance of a complaint to be dealt with informally

*To the complainant*

Society of Independent Practitioners, 3 Roundway House
Leicester LE5 6BA

Confidential

Please contact me at
Rose House
6 Corner Lane
London W10 5BC                                                              date

Dear John Smith,

The Complaints Committee of the Society met on —— and has
accepted your complaint against Barbara West. It has suggested that
the matter be dealt with in the first case informally and we are
suggesting that —— be the conciliator. Should he/she not be
acceptable to you because you do not feel that he/she will be impartial
will you please contact me?

This meeting will be held on ——/I will be contacting you within
the next week to arrange a date for the meeting.

Please send all communications to the above address.

Yours sincerely,


Ann Paul
Chair of the Complaints Committee

*To the complained against*

> Society of Independent Practitioners, 3 Roundway House
> Leicester LE5 6BA

Confidential

Please contact me at
Rose House
6 Corner Lane
London W10 5BC                                                          date

Dear Barbara West,

The Complaints Committee of the Society met on ―― and has accepted the complaint made by John Smith against you. It has suggested that the matter be dealt with in the first case informally.

This meeting will be held on ―― / I will be contacting you within the next week to arrange a date. The conciliator will be ―― . Should he/she not be acceptable to you because you do not feel that he/she will be impartial will you please contact me?

Please send all communications to the above address.

Yours sincerely,


Ann Paul
Chair of the Complaints Committee


## Notice of an informal meeting

> Society of Independent Practitioners, 3 Roundway House
> Leicester LE5 6BA

Confidential

Please contact me at
Rose House
6 Corner Lane
London W10 5BC                                                          date

Dear ―― ,

This letter is to confirm that the meeting to discuss the complaint by John Smith against Barbara West will be held on ―― at ―― (plus any special arrangements).

The meeting is informal, and is being arranged in order to see if there is any room for mediation or conciliation between the parties. Please contact me about the outcome of the meeting by ——— .

Yours sincerely,


Ann Paul
Chair of the Complaints Committee

## Letters informing parties of the outcome of an informal meeting

Society of Independent Practitioners, 3 Roundway House
Leicester LE5 6BA

Confidential

Please contact me at
Rose House
6 Corner Lane
London W10 5BC                                                              date

Dear John Smith/Barbara West,

Mary Jones met you on ——— and has reported to the Complaints Committee that the outcome of the meeting with Barbara West, John Smith and her was satisfactory.
   I am very glad that these matters are now resolved.

Yours sincerely,


Ann Paul
Chair of the Complaints Committee

Society of Independent Practitioners, 3 Roundway House
Leicester LE5 6BA

Confidential

Please contact me at
Rose House,
6 Corner Lane
London W10 5BC                                                    date

Dear Barbara West/John Smith,

Mary Jones met you on ⎯⎯ and has reported to the Complaints Committee the outcome of your meeting. It has been decided that the matter should now be taken up as a formal complaint.

I will be contacting you within ⎯⎯ days with a date for the investigation meeting/ the adjudication meeting.

Yours sincerely,


Ann Paul
Chair of the Complaints Committee


## Notice of an investigation meeting

Society of Independent Practitioners, 3 Roundway House
Leicester LE5 6BA

Confidential

Please contact me at
Rose House
6 Corner Lane
London W10 5BC                                                    date

Dear ⎯⎯ ,

This letter is to confirm that the meeting to investigate the complaint by John Smith against Barbara West will be held on ⎯⎯ at ⎯⎯ (plus any special arrangements).

Please send any submissions to me at the above address fourteen working days before the date of the meeting, that is by ⎯⎯ . I will be sending you John Smith's/Barbara West's submissions five working days before the meeting.

A member of the complaints committee will be on hand to meet you when you arrive at ——.

Yours sincerely,


Ann Paul
Chair of the Complaints Committee

## Letter to external consultant and members of an investigation or adjudication

Society of Independent Practitioners, 3 Roundway House
Leicester LE5 6BA

Confidential

Please contact me at
Rose House
6 Corner Lane
London W10 5BC                                                                 date

Dear ——,

The Complaints Committee of the society met on —— and has accepted the complaint made by John Smith against Barbara West. It has suggested that the matter be dealt with in the first case informally/by investigation/by a formal adjudication. Thank you for agreeing to act as a conciliator/an investigator/an adjudicator. Please let me know if there is any reason which might compromise your impartiality.

This meeting will be held on —— / I will be contacting you within the next week to arrange a date. I will be sending you the papers at least five working days before that date.

Please communicate with me only through the above address.

Yours sincerely,


Ann Paul
Chair of the Complaints Committee

## Letters to inform the parties of the outcome of an investigation

*Asking for responses to the report*

Society of Independent Practitioners, 3 Roundway House
Leicester LE5 6BA

Confidential

Please contact me at
Rose House
6 Corner Lane
London W10 5BC                                              date

Dear John Smith/Barbara West,

<u>Complaint by John Smith against Barbara West</u>

Two copies of the report of the Investigation carried out by Mary Jones are enclosed. Please read the report and you may, if you wish, return one annotated copy to me within ten working days. The Complaints Committee will be meeting on ―― to consider the report. I will write to you within a week of this to inform you of its decision.

Yours sincerely,


Ann Paul
Chair of the Complaints Committee

*When the matter is resolved*

> Society of Independent Practitioners, 3 Roundway House
> Leicester LE5 6BA

Confidential

Please contact me at
Rose House
6 Corner Lane
London W10 5BC                                                    date

Dear John Smith/Barbara West,

### Complaint by John Smith against Barbara West

The Complaints Committee of the Society met on ____ and thoroughly considered the investigator's report and your responses.

The Committee believes that this matter should be stopped and go no further. You have the right to appeal against this decision and have thirty-one days in which to do so.

Yours sincerely,


Ann Paul
Chair of the Complaints Committee


*When the matter is not resolved*

> Society of Independent Practitioners, 3 Roundway House
> Leicester LE5 6BA

Confidential

Please contact me at
Rose House
6 Corner Lane
London W10 5BC                                                    date

Dear John Smith/Barbara West,

### Complaint by John Smith against Barbara West

The Complaints Committee of the Society met on ____ and thoroughly considered the Investigator's report and your responses.

The Committee now believe that this matter should proceed to adjudication.

The adjudication meeting will be held on ⸺ at ⸺ / I will be contacting you within the next week to arrange a date for this meeting. The names of the adjudication panel will be George Osowski and Janet McGregor from the Society and Tre Patel from the Association. Should any of these people be unacceptable to you because you do not believe that they are impartial will you please contact me immediately?

Please make sure that I have your full submissions fourteen working days before the adjudication date in order that they may be duplicated and distributed to the panel.

Yours sincerely,


Ann Paul
Chair of the Complaints Committee


## Letters to confirm the adjudication meeting did not uphold the complaint

*To the complainant*

> Society of Independent Practitioners, 3 Roundway House
> Leicester LE5 6BA

Confidential – addressee only

Please contact me at
Rose House
6 Corner Lane
London W10 5BC                                                    date

Dear John Smith,

### Complaint by John Smith against Barbara West

The Adjudication Panel decided after their meeting with you on ⸺ that your complaint against Barbara West was not substantiated. It has therefore, been decided that the matter will proceed no further.

We understand that you brought this complaint believing that you had good cause; and we believe that you will understand the reasons for our decision.

You have thirty days in which to appeal against this decision if you wish to do so, that would mean by ⸺ .

The Society does not condone breaches of confidentiality in matters relating to information that you may have received during the processing of this complaint.

We would ask you to maintain the close confidentiality that you have observed until now.

Yours sincerely,


Ann Paul
Chair of the Complaints Committee


*To the practitioner*

Society of Independent Practitioners, 3 Roundway House
Leicester LE5 6BA

Confidential – addressee only

Please contact me at
Rose House
6 Corner Lane
London W10 5BC                                                              date

Dear Barbara West

### Complaint by John Smith against Barbara West

The Adjudication Panel decided after their meeting with you on ——
that the complaint against you was not substantiated. It has therefore, been decided that the matter will proceed no further.

John Smith has thirty days in which to appeal against this decision, i.e. by ——.

The Society does not condone breaches of confidentiality in matters relating to information that you may have received during the processing of this complaint.

We would ask you to maintain the close confidentiality that you have observed until now.

Yours sincerely,


Ann Paul
Chair of the Complaints Committee

## Letters if the complaint is upheld

*To the complainant*

> Society of Independent Practitioners, 3 Roundway House
> Leicester LE5 6BA

Confidential – addressee only

Please contact me at
Rose House
6 Corner Lane
London W10 5BC                                                          date

Dear John Smith,

<u>Complaint by John Smith against Barbara West</u>

The Adjudication Panel decided after its meeting with you on ──
that the complaint made by you was upheld on the following grounds:
1
2

In the light of this the following sanctions will be recommended to
the Board of the Society.
1
2

Should you wish to appeal against these decisions or sanctions you
have seven days in which to do so, by the ──. Any letter of appeal
should be addressed to the Chair of the Society at the following
address ──.

The Society does not condone breaches of confidentiality in
matters relating to information that you may have received during the
processing of this complaint.

We would ask you to maintain the close confidentiality that you
have observed until now.

Yours sincerely,

Ann Paul
Chair of the Complaints Committee

*To the practitioner*

Society of Independent Practitioners, 3 Roundway House
Leicester LE5 6BA

Confidential – addressee only

Please contact me at
Rose House
6 Corner Lane
London W10 5BC                                                       date

Dear Barbara West,

### Complaint by John Smith against Barbara West

The Adjudication Panel decided after its meeting with you on ——
that the complaint against you was upheld on the following grounds:
1
2

In the light of this the following sanctions will be recommended to
the Board of the Society
1
2

Should you wish to appeal against these decisions or sanctions you
have seven days in which to do so, i.e. by the —— . Any letter of
appeal should be addressed to the Chair of the Society at the
following address —— .

The Society does not condone breaches of confidentiality in
matters relating to information that you may have received during the
processing of this complaint.

We would ask you to maintain the close confidentiality that you
have observed until now.

Yours sincerely,


Ann Paul
Chair of the Complaints Committee

## To the parties to the complaint once the time for appeal has expired

Society of Independent Practitioners, 3 Roundway House
Leicester LE5 6BA

Confidential – addressee only

Please contact me at
Rose House
6 Corner Lane
London W10 5BC                                                                date

Dear John Smith/Barbara West,

Complaint by John Smith against Barbara West

In the above matter Barbara West/John Smith has not appealed against the decision of the adjudication panel.

Yours sincerely,


Ann Paul
Chair of the Complaints Committee


## If an appeal is made

Society of Independent Practitioners, 3 Roundway House
Leicester LE5 6BA

Confidential – addressee only

Please contact me at
Rose House
6 Corner Lane
London W10 5BC                                                                date

Dear John Smith/Barbara West,

Complaint by John Smith against Barbara West

In the above matter Barbara West/John Smith has appealed against the decision of the adjudication panel. The appeal will be heard by ____ and ____ on ____ . I will write to you within a week of this about the outcome.

Yours sincerely,


Richard Short
Chair of the Board

## Notice of the decision of the Appeals Panel

*If the appeal is not upheld*

> Society of Independent Practitioners, 3 Roundway House
> Leicester LE5 6BA

Confidential – addressee only

Please contact me at
Rose House
6 Corner Lane
London W10 5BC                                                                date

Dear John Smith/Barbara West,

<u>Complaint by John Smith against Barbara West</u>

The Appeal Panel decided after its meeting on —— that the complaint against you/Barbara West was not upheld on the following grounds:
1
2
3

    This matter is accordingly now closed.

Yours sincerely,


Richard Short
Chair of the Board

*Or if the appeal is upheld*

Society of Independent Practitioners, 3 Roundway House
Leicester LE5 6BA

Confidential – addressee only

Please contact me at
Rose House
6 Corner Lane
London W10 5BC          date

Dear John Smith/Barbara West,

<u>Complaint by John Smith against Barbara West</u>

The Appeal Panel decided after its meeting on _____ that the complaint against you/Barbara West was upheld on the following grounds:

1
2
3

The matter will be taken up at paragraph X point Y of the Complaints Procedure.

Ann Paul will be in touch with you in the next few days.

Yours sincerely,


Richard Short
Chair of the Board

# Index

'LIBRARY, UNIVERSITY COLLEGE CHESTER